SIX DAYS TO BETTER GOLF

A GOLF MAGAZINE BOOK

Preface by Ken Venturi

DRAWINGS BY DOM LUPO

SIX DAYS TO BETTER GOLF

THE SECRET OF LEARNING THE GOLF SWING

By Harry Obitz
and Dick Farley

With Desmond Tolhurst

HARPER & ROW, PUBLISHERS, NEW YORK
CAMBRIDGE, PHILADELPHIA, SAN FRANCISCO, WASHINGTON
LONDON, MEXICO CITY, SÃO PAULO, SINGAPORE, SYDNEY

Harry Obitz and Dick Farley dedicate this book
to the 5:42 Club, who need it.

PICTURE CREDITS: Pages 10–11, 21, 43, 57, 87, 172—Desmond Tolhurst; pages 92, 94, 158, 161, 162, 164—Leonard Kamsler, Golf Magazine; page 106—Author's collection.

This is a 1988 reissue of a book first published by Harper & Row in 1977.

Library of Congress Cataloging in Publication Data

Obitz, Harry.
    Six days to better golf.
    "A Golf magazine book."
    1. Swing (Golf) I. Farley, Dick, joint author.
II. Tolhurst, Desmond, joint author. III. Title.
GV979.S9024 1977   796.352'3   76-9196
ISBN 0-06-013203-5

88 89 90 91 92 HC 10 9 8 7 6 5 4 3 2 1

Contents

Preface

Swinging the golf club has always been the key to winning championships. A good golf swing gives you the rhythm, tempo and balance that enables your game to stand up to all conditions and the tremendous pressure of competitive golf. The true swinging action is in fact the "groove" that keeps you going even when the pressure becomes a major factor. The true swing is also the only basis for acquiring the different shots necessary for a well-rounded game. I'm known as a good shot-maker, but I would never have been able to learn these shots without first learning the fundamentals of a good golf swing.

That is why it is my pleasure to write a preface for this book by Harry Obitz and Dick Farley. Harry and Dick have been teaching the pure golf swing for many years. And in this book they have done an outstanding job in clearly presenting the way to learn to swing the club. They tell you what it's all about, and what it isn't, and what's more important, they show you how to acquire the feel of a good golf swing for yourself. They show you the way to build a good golf swing from scratch, or rebuild a faulty one.

Their emphasis on the importance of "swing" is why I think all golfers should read this book. Whether you're a beginner or experienced player, you'll find a wealth of knowledge in these pages.

Ken Venturi, *1964 U.S. Open Champion*

Introduction

When my old friends Harry Obitz and Dick Farley asked me to write a few lines to tee off this book, my first reaction was, Why? After all, I said, I'm neither a famed player nor a well-known personality; I'm just a golf writer.

Harry and Dick wouldn't accept that. They pointed out that I started playing golf when I was 10 years old and have been studying the game for over 30 years. I have been writing instruction articles for Golf Magazine on and off for the last 15 years and also for other national golf publications on a free-lance basis when working for the USGA and for what was then known as the PGA Tournament Players Division. During this period I have been exposed to more golf theories and instructional ideas than most golfers hear in a lifetime. Also, in writing these articles I have worked with many of the greatest golfers and greatest teachers of our time. All of this experience, Harry and Dick thought, qualified me to put their "Swing's the Thing" method into perspective. Here goes.

The big difference between Obitz and Farley and any other teacher currently on the national scene is their insistence on the importance of the true swing. And by "swing" Harry and Dick don't mean just any sort of action that moves a golf ball. To them a true swinging action is a specific type of action, the one action you must have if you want to play good golf.

As they point out, there are many, many ways in which you can move a golf club. You can push it, pull it, heave with it, sway with it, lift it and hack down with it, to name just a few, but the only way to obtain effortless power with consistency and good direction is to swing.

Obitz and Farley recognize that what separates the weekend golfer from the great players is that all great players truly swing the club; the weekend golfer does not. That's why Harry and Dick insisted that, whatever might or might not be included in this book, we had to cover, and cover thoroughly, every aspect of "swing." In their own teaching, they first impress on the pupil the importance of the true swing and second, use every method they know to teach the pupil how to acquire a true swinging action. That, briefly, is the scheme of this book.

The true swinging action, ironically, is the one element that receives short shrift in modern golf instruction. And there is a very simple reason for this. Whether the professional is a top player or top teacher, he learned a swinging action so long ago that he takes it for granted and assumes his readers, too, have mastered what he considers basic.

This assumption is false. Even great golfers lose their swings occasionally. Weekend golfers play well when they swing better than usual, and play badly when they don't swing, but they never realize that the presence or absence of a swinging action is the reason for their inconsistency. It would not be putting the matter too strongly to state that 90 percent of all golfers have no clear understanding of the word "swing."

At present, there are two ways you can learn the Obitz/Farley "Swing's the Thing" method. One way is to go to the golf schools they run for Golf Magazine. These courses last six days and cost the better part of $1,000. The second way costs roughly a hundredth of that sum and it is, of course, to work with the material in this book.

At the schools the curriculum is organized in the following fashion: Day One—Understanding the true swinging action and learning the static fundamentals such as the correct hold, alignment, posture and the tilt; Day Two—Learning the upswing of the arms with the turn of the shoulders; Day Three—Learning the downswing of the arms and the release of the right side; Day Four—Blending the upswing and downswing, learning to time the swing, developing correct tempo; Day Five—Continuing work on blending the upswing and downswing into one continuous movement, understanding the flight of the ball and how it applies to the swing; and Day Six—More blending the swing, with work on specialized shots.

You should follow the same general plan in working with this book (hence the title *Six Days to Better Golf*). You must understand what a swinging action is before you attempt to build or rebuild your swing. You have to learn the static principles of the correct set before attempting the quarter-swing. You should master the quarter-swing before advancing to the half-, three-quarter, or full swing. You must learn the full swing before advancing to shotmaking. And so on.

One thing Obitz and Farley promise you: If you work conscientiously with this book, you will learn the true swinging action. In so doing you will have taken that first and most vital step toward playing the game the way the champions play it.

Desmond Tolhurst

1
"The Swing's the Thing"

JUST ABOUT EVERY GOLFER who comes to us for "the secret" of the golf swing thinks of the swing as a succession of individual movements he must make with various parts of his body. To help him in his quest for the perfect golf action, he tries to "take it back low and slow," "keep his left arm straight," "turn his left shoulder under his chin," "cock his wrists," "start the downswing with the left knee"—or both knees, or whatever.

The result is, of course, confusion. It's impossible to focus attention on so many different parts of the body during an action that takes less than two seconds to complete. However, it is simple, as you will learn, to concentrate on swinging the hands and the club with the forearms.

The mistake that golfers make is to confuse cause with effect. The straight left arm, full shoulder turn, etc., do not create the swing; they are the *results* of using a true swinging action.

This is why we have, for many years now, devoted ourselves—in our personal teaching, in print, and in our golf show—to the proposition that "The Swing's the Thing." The true swinging action is the only way to move the club for maximum efficiency, as regards both distance and direction. It's one indivisible, continuous live action—not little bits and pieces.

1

A tiger is a beautiful creature. It moves with grace and spring. But you can't find the secret of its action by dissecting it. You will have "pieces of tiger" but no "tiger."

The "Swing Weight"

What then is a swing? It has a definite form: circular. It produces centrifugal force.

That centrifugal force is what it's all about. When you have centrifugal force, you are developing the most powerful and repeating action a human being is capable of. And you are making a true swing.

One doesn't have to be an Einstein to appreciate centrifugal force. If, as a child, you ever played with a sling—the type David used to kill Goliath—you'll know the power of centrifugal force. If you haven't done that, well, we're certain that at some time or other you've tied a stone or other weight to a length of string and then whirled it around your hand.

Studying the action of the "Swing Weight" teaches you the principles of the true swing in golf. It demonstrates the power and repeating groove of a centrifugal force action.

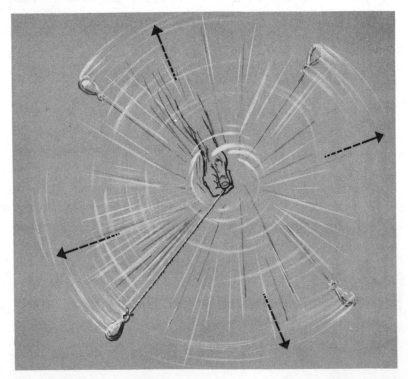

Let's study the action of the weight on the string for a moment. It can teach us many of the principles of the true swing in golf. A three-foot length of string is about right; the weight can be just about anything, as long as you can tie the string securely to it! (We call this the "Swing Weight" because it's so useful in explaining the swing to our pupils.)

Ready? Hold the end of the string and then get the weight swinging in a circle. You'll notice that you can get terrific speed into the weight with only a slight movement in the hand and forearm. Very little effort as such is necessary. However, to get the weight swinging, the application of force must be gradual and smooth. If you make sudden, jerky movements, the weight slows down, falls out of its "groove," and in fact stops swinging. (Now you can see why conscious efforts to put "punch" into a shot so often result in a mishit.)

Moral: When your golf action is a true swing, the weight of the swinging club creates both the repeating groove you need and all the power at your command.

The Role of the Forearm

Another thing you'll notice as you swing the "Swing Weight" is that the forearm-to-hand area initiates the swing. You are aware of the pull of the centrifugal force generated by the weight in your fingers as you whirl it around, but, to keep it swinging, the best point of concentration is the *forearm*.

Actually, we can be more precise than that. If you'll stop the weight's swinging a moment, we'll bet that you are holding the end of the string between your thumb and forefinger; it is here that your "feel" of the action is. This is as it should be. The thumbs and forefingers of both hands are the "feelers" in the grip, and the rest of the fingers are the "grabbers" or holders of the club.

The forearm enters the picture as soon as you start swinging the weight again. Once you get it swinging, speed up the swing a bit. You'll feel immediately what we mean. It's the forearm that's accentuating the speed of the swing.

While we're analyzing the action in the forearm-to-hand area, we would like to make another point. We'll bet that the whole time that you have been swinging the weight, you have never been conscious of what your wrist was doing. In fact, it was simply reacting to the action. Again, this is as it should be: You should never use your wrists consciously in swinging a weight of any description, including a golf club.

To prove this to yourself, all you have to do is get the "Swing Weight" swinging and then try to swing it by conscious application of the wrists. Before you know it, the weight will have slowed down and you will have lost the swinging motion.

Why do we make such a point of concentrating on the action of the forearm-to-hand area? Well, just about every teacher in the world will tell you that you have to have a swinging action, one that develops centrifugal force. *But not one in a hundred will tell you how to do it!* Before you know it, you're enmeshed in "bits and pieces" instruction—and you're lost.

The late Ernest Jones (our good friend, by the way) at least tried to impart the feel of a good swing to his pupils. Ernie used to say, "Swing the clubhead, and you can forget everything else." If it were that simple, however, there would be far more single-figure handicap golfers around. Ernie also used to say, "Swing the clubhead with your hands." We would agree with the *principle* behind Ernie's method—that the true swing is what is important, not "bits and pieces" tips—but we have found that "Swing the clubhead" and "Swing the clubhead with the hands" seldom produce a good swing.

Too many golfers—we have seen thousands of these cases—get the wrong idea from "Swing the clubhead." They somehow imagine that *the clubhead is going to swing them* instead of the other way around. The resulting action is often pretty, but it's always powerless. The club is "dropped" *on* the ball—it's not swung *powerfully through the ball*, as it should be. "Swing the clubhead" players too often produce what we call a "pattycake" action reminiscent of ladies' tennis back in the Victorian era. It's of no use at all. This is the 20th century, and women and men alike must learn to swing the club as forcefully as they can if they want power in their game.

The second problem with Ernie's ideas—now we're referring to the concept of swinging the clubhead with the hands—is that if you concentrate on the hands, the hands and wrists become far too active at the start of the backswing. The golfer either "drags" the clubhead away, with the wrists and hands leading the clubhead away from the ball, or he or she lifts the clubhead up quickly with the hands and wrists. *Neither of these actions is a true swinging action.* And if you don't begin with a swinging action, it makes it almost impossible to swing later.

Actually, these dragging or lifting actions are a form of leverage. To see this, swing the weight again and notice that, when the weight is swinging freely, the hand and weight are traveling in the same direction. They must do this if you want a true swing. Now try to move the weight with an opposite movement of the hand. The swing jerks to a stop. Yet golfers, mistakenly, will introduce some form of leverage into the swing, where the hands and clubhead move in different directions!

The thought of swinging the clubhead with the hands also hurts the downswing. What happens is that the golfer tries to speed the clubhead up with the hands. This can result in "throwing from the top," in which the golfer releases the wrist and arm cock as the first move of the downswing, so the power of the swing is lost by the time the clubhead reaches the ball. It can also result in a misguided effort to whip the clubhead through the ball with the hands; this actually slows down the action and destroys the swing.

You can prove this to yourself by swinging the "Swing Weight" and seeing what happens if you apply force consciously with your hand. Get the weight swinging again and gradually increase the speed of swing to your maximum. Then try for more speed. You'll find that when your hand gets into the act and tries to move the weight faster, what happens is that, although the hand goes faster, the weight has "fallen" out of the swing—the swing in fact is destroyed.

Remember: You can move a club with a faster or a slower swinging action as long as your forearms are calling the shots, swinging the hands via responsive wrists, but you can't move the clubhead faster than you can swing it. When you try to do so by making the hands active, you destroy the swing.

At the other end of the scale from "Swing the clubhead," we remember some years ago a British doctor who keyed his whole swing theory on feeling the action of the swing in his left shoulder. To our way of thinking that's really making things difficult. Not that the action of the shoulders is unimportant (we'll have a lot to say about them later in this book), but to key the whole swing on the left shoulder is to key on something too remote from the action. The lower arms, the hands, and the club are where the action is.

Don't "Force" the Swing

If you get the "Swing Weight" swinging again with the forearm, and then transfer the motivation for the swing to the upper arm or shoulder, you will see quite clearly what can and often does happen to "shoulder" players. Those big muscles start pushing and pulling, and they jerk the swing from its center and slow it to a halt. The same thing happens in the golf swing.

Moral: The big muscles of the body must *respond* to the swing and move in sympathy with the swing, but you shouldn't use them to motivate a swinging action. They'll just overpower and destroy it.

Here's another point from our "Swing Weight": You'll notice that the forefinger and thumb are not the center of the swing. Your whole arm is continually on the move, the forearm generating the swing and the upper arm moving in sympathy with it. In the same way, in the golf swing the hands are not the center, or zero point, of the swing. The centrifugal force you generate will find, via the hands and arms, a center or zero point somewhere in your body. Of course, you can't swing with the zero point, because it doesn't move. That's why we advocate swinging the hands with the forearms. But awareness of the zero point can be useful in the golf swing, which is on a larger scale than our demonstration here with the weight on a string.

We have observed, by means of our swinging weight, that the arc of a swing never changes, provided it remains a swing. However, this does not mean that the swing cannot be changed in any way, as has been maintained by some teachers (including Ernie Jones).

First, you can swing at a faster or slower tempo, as we've just seen. Just as important, you can open the clubface and produce a slice or close the clubface and produce a hook. Just because you're opening or closing the clubface doesn't mean that you have to stop swinging. And the same thing applies to the path of the swing. You can swing through the ball from inside the target line to outside, or from outside to inside, or you can swing it more upright or flat and still be swinging.

We'll get into the mechanics of modifying the swing to produce different shots later in this book. For now, we want to make the point that the forearm-to-hand area is the most important in the production of the true swing. Once you can make a true swing, you can then advance to learning how to hit different types of shots by simple changes of the plane and arc of the swing.

The Swing Is for Men and Women

In concluding this chapter we would like to give the last word to the ladies. All we have said applies equally to men and women. In fact—forgive us for observing—it goes double for women. Since you are not, as a general rule, as strong as men, you can only produce satisfactory results if your golf swing more nearly approaches perfection. Men can get some sort of shot away by "muscling" the ball with the upper arms and shoulders (in our book, that's exerting leverage); but for women, that shot would go nowhere.

Pound for pound, the top LPGA tour players have better swings than all but the best—and we mean the best—of the male tourers. They have to.

For men, there's a moral here. We know you identify more with a Nicklaus or a Miller than, say, a Palmer (we mean Sandra, not Arnie). But don't fail to watch the women tour players; you'll see some of the purest swings around. This has always been so. We can remember seeing the great Joyce Wethered play. Of her, Bobby Jones (the only man to win the Grand Slam) said: "She has the greatest golf swing of all, *man or woman.*"

Then there was Babe Zaharias. She used to "slug" or muscle the ball when she first learned the game. But she played her best golf once she realized what the swing truly is. And Mickey Wright—there's another great one. If ever there was a distaff equivalent of a Nicklaus, she was it. She has awesome power, and it's all produced by a free swinging action—our credo for over 40 years.

Obitz and Farley Say:

1. The golf swing is not a series of parts; it's an entity, a specific type of action.

2. The true swing—a free swinging action—makes everything else happen. It's the "groove" of the swing. It makes such "parts" as wrist action, shoulder turn, and leg action happen automatically.

3. The true swing is motivated by the forearms swinging the hands and club via the medium of reactive wrists. It is not motivated by the hands swinging the clubhead or by the body.

4. If you make a true swing, you are making the most powerful repeating action you are capable of. Any other type of action is less efficient; either it moves the club slower (less power) or it's less consistent (no longer in the "groove").

5. *The Swing's the Thing!*

2

Learning the Swing

IN THE PRECEDING CHAPTER we learned that a true swinging action is the action most desired in golf. We also learned what a swing is, how to feel and produce it, and what prevents or stops a swinging action (leverage). Now we will apply the same principles to learning to swing a golf club.

In the full golf swing, you swing the club back until you have made a full turn with the shoulders and the arms have swung the club up until the hands are about over the right shoulder. And then you swing down and through the ball. But what mechanism changes directions in the swing? What prevents you from swinging back forever and never getting back to the ball? Do you have to make a conscious move to start the downswing?

It's been our observation that not 10 golfers in 100 know the answers to those questions, or, if they know the right answers in theory, they can't achieve the correct change of direction in practice.

In many ways, the change of direction is the nemesis for the average golfer. Typically he turns his hips as much as his shoulders (this is known as "spinning" the hips) and has to make a conscious move to bring the club down—we'll tell you right now that's the wrong way to do it—or else he never turns his shoulders enough and has to heave at the ball solely with his upper arms and shoulders—and you know by now that leverage exerted by the upper arms and shoulders is not going to produce a swinging action!

The answer to our questions is quite simple: It's a principle we call "coil/recoil" and it works in pretty much the same way as flicking a rubber band.

We're sure you remember the first time you got your hands on a rubber band. And the use you saw for it was not for keeping your papers tidy! What you did was to wrap one end round a thumb, pull back on the end with your forefinger and thumb, and then release it at any target that took your fancy. Remember the power you got with that simple device? Well, the same thing happens in a good golf swing.

How Coil/Recoil Works in the Swing

When you set up to the ball, you brace both knees inward a little so that you set up resistance in the legs to the windup in the shoulders and hips. The coiling action starts as the forearms swing the hands and club and the arms back together, because the shoulders start turning in response to the arm swing and this action begins to wind up the muscles in the left side of the back and this pulls the hips around. The turning of the hips pulls the left knee back and behind the ball, the left foot rolls inward, and, in a full swing, the left heel may be pulled slightly from the ground. At the change of direction in the swing, the hips are the first to reach their maximum turn, usually around 45 degrees on a full swing. Then the shoulders complete their turn, which should be around 90 degrees on a full swing (more if the player is supple). Then the arms complete their upswing and the wrists complete their "cocking" action.

The downswing is started in the same way as the backswing, by the arms swinging down. Slightly after that the recoil of the body takes place. In the backswing, the coil began at the top with the shoulders and progressed downward to the hips, the legs, and the footwork. In the downswing, the recoil starts from the bottom up. As the hips completed their turn, the right leg still held firm; the right knee remained flexed, preventing any lateral movement. There was also some tension in the left leg, which was pulled around by the hip turn. The body was in much the same position as the rubber band pulled to its limit; the shoulders were fully wound up against the resistance set up in the legs. Something, of course, has to give. The legs are forced to release, driving to the left and pulling the hips and then the shoulders around. Meanwhile, the arms have continued to swing down, and the arm swing and

A

The "chair" exercise shows how coil/ recoil works in the golf swing. Sit toward the edge of a chair to perform an imaginary swing without a club (A). Swing the arms back freely, allowing the shoulders to turn as fully as possible. Note the pull in the muscles in the left side of the back (B). Just after the arms start their downward swing, the legs will recoil, driving to the left, and the arms will whip through the ball (C).

body coordinate in a free-wheeling, flailing action through the ball.

Although this description of how you coil the upper body against the resistance of the lower body in the backswing and recoil in the downswing was necessarily rather detailed, you can prove the basic simplicity of the idea by the following exercise.

Sit toward the edge of a regular chair (not a swiveling chair) and imagine that you are going to drive a golf ball from that position. In other words, you'll swing without a club. Just swing the arms back as freely as you can and allow the shoulders to turn as much as possible in response to the arm swing. The first thing you'll feel is a pull in the muscles in the left side of the back. Then, suddenly, you'll find that you've swung through the ball. What happened? Swing the arms back again, but this time take your eyes off the imaginary ball and watch your legs. Observe that just after the arms start to swing down, the legs recoil with the left knee driving left and the right knee a split second after it.

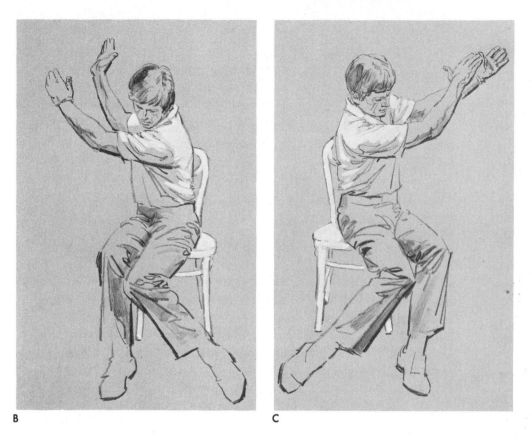

B   C

And a split second after that you'll see the arms whipping through the "ball."

This chair exercise is, of course, a slight exaggeration of what happens in the golf swing, but it will give you the feel of the coil/recoil. This is vitally important; so many golfers never learn it and as a result are condemned to a flabby, powerless action.

Basically there are three reasons for this: The first is that many golfers are self-taught and never hear about coil/recoil. Second, a lot of golfers were taught some sort of swinging action first, and the principle of coil/recoil was only explained later. Third, many golfers are taught the full swing with a wood first.

Concerning the first reason there is little to say. A self-taught golfer is invariably a bad golfer. The few exceptions to that rule—such as Sam Snead—only prove that with exceptional physical talent and a good model (in Sam's case, his elder brother Homer) you can learn to play this game. Most golfers just don't have Sam's talent.

About the second reason: We've never agreed that coil/recoil is something that can be added after the basic swing is learned. Once a pupil has learned to swing back without any resistance in the legs, it becomes doubly difficult for him or her to learn coil/recoil. Why? Because any faulty action learned in golf (or any other sport) has to be *unlearned* before the right action can be acquired. This takes time. We think it is far easier for you to understand and learn to incorporate coil/recoil from the start.

The third reason, that the full swing with a wood is taught first, is not entirely the fault of the instructor. Long hitting has always been exciting to golfers of both sexes. To watch a Jack Nicklaus or a Tom Weiskopf or a Jim Dent or a JoAnne Carner or a Mickey Wright hit the long ball is thrilling. So the pupil practically insists on learning the full swing first. But what these golfers don't know is that any full swing—even a raw, faulty beginner's swing—will generate some centrifugal force. And, frankly, beginners are not up to controlling such force or such a big movement. Their swings have no automatic controls such as a proper "set" or address position. Moreover, in the full swing, the club goes behind you—out of sight and, for a beginner or inexperienced player, out of control. The player becomes obsessed with learning the correct backswing, and in efforts to do so, he or she completely ignores the rather obvious fact that the ball is struck as the club swings through. Thus coil/recoil, even if it has been taught to the pupil, probably gets lost in the shuffle. Since there's no coil, there's no recoil—and no automatic thrust of the legs in the downswing.

Start with a Quarter-swing

To learn the swing most easily, we believe that the golfer should start with quarter-swings, then progress through half-swings and three-quarter swings to the full swing. In this way the golfer is building on a solid foundation.

The players who learn the full swing first—and especially those who learn it with a driver—usually have difficulty with the short game. They chop at the ball instead of swinging *through* it. With our method, the closer you get to the green, the more confident you'll feel.

We teach all our pupils by this method and have done so for years. Harry Obitz has been teaching by this method since 1931, when he turned pro, and Dick Farley since 1950, when he came East to join Harry at Shawnee. Funnily enough, many other professionals have said that ideally a pupil should learn the short swings first and progress to longer swings, but as far as we know *not many of them did anything about it*—it remained just an "impossible dream."

Start Practicing the Swing with a 7-iron

We believe strongly that you must start the learning process with a club that is easy to handle. Our pupils learn the basic swinging motion with a 7-iron. This is the ideal club to learn with because it's long enough so that you can learn a true swinging motion, yet it's not so long—as a wood would be, for example—that it generates too much centrifugal force for the inexperienced golfer to control. It also has the merit of having plenty of loft. The last thing we want our pupils to do is to "help" the ball up in the air. The 7-iron's generous loft is a great aid to confidence, so there's no "scooping," but instead a free swing through the ball.

And, as we said earlier, we would start you with short, partial swings and work you up gradually to the full swing. This applies not only to beginners, but to more experienced golfers who, for whatever reason, have not learned a true swing. You've got to learn the twin concepts of swing and coil/recoil in a format that you can comfortably perform and, at the same time, build up your confidence by striking the ball solidly from the beginning. We will even put good golfers right through the Obitz/Farley swing learning system so that they have a full understanding of it. In their case, of course, we can advance them more quickly.

Now we want to explain the swing and coil/recoil a little further. The description we gave earlier in this chapter was in fact a "once over lightly" treatment, even though it might have appeared complex at first. We deliberately didn't make a complete explanation of the swing at that time because we wanted you to feel for yourself in the chair exercise how the arm swing and body coordinate. Once you have that feeling in your system you are ready to understand fully what makes the golf swing tick.

There are two factors to the golf swing—two working parts, if you like. The first is the arms. *The arms make the swing.* The arms swing the club up and down, and in so doing they set the *plane* of the swing and the *speed* of the swing. The second factor or working part of the swing is the body. *The body times the swing and it does this by means of the coil/recoil action.* The complete golf swing is really a combination of timing the arm swing with the body action.

The Role of the Arms

Let's explain the term "arm swing" at this point. As we've said, the forearms motivate the swing. However, the end result of the forearm action is to swing both arms, and since the hands and the club are attached to the arms, the term "arm swing" includes not only the arms themselves but the free swinging action they generate in the hands and the club via the medium of the wrists.

How does the arm swing set the plane? The principle we have always stood for is that, in the pure swing, you always have some latitude in swinging the arms. When you've got the club set behind the ball, you can decide whether you are going to make the swing flatter by swinging the arms on a more horizontal plane or more upright by swinging the arms in a more nearly vertical path.

But there are limits to varying the plane of the arm swing for a normal swing. We don't advocate swinging the arms any lower than a position in which the hands at the top of the swing would be at a point above the right shoulder—that's the flattest normal swing we recommend. As for the limits of uprightness in the arm swing, we think the highest you should go would be a point at which the hands at the top of the swing are halfway between the right shoulder and the neck.

The *normal* swing plane for a regular swing for you, as an individual, will depend on your stature and physique. A tall, slender player like Dick Farley will swing his arms up to a point between the right shoulder and the neck on his normal swing. A shorter, thickset golfer like Harry Obitz will normally swing his arms up more over the right shoulder. In order to get a successful blend of arm swing and body action, your normal swing plane should be between a point over the right shoulder and one midway between the shoulder and the neck. We won't cut it finer than that because there's always room for some individuality in the swing.

The arm swing also is responsible for the speed of the swing. And you control the speed of the swing by the tempo with which you swing the arms. If you swing the arms back fast and you control it with the full coil and a full swing, you're going to hit the ball with your maximum power. At the other end of the tempo spectrum, you can swing the arms at a slower speed to take some of the power out of the swing.

Whereas the arms swing in a semi-vertical plane, the body operates almost on a horizontal plane. In other words, the action of the shoulders, body, and legs in the golf swing is essentially the same as in a baseball swing, where the shoulders and hips work in a horizontal plane, except that in golf your back is somewhat tilted forward to compensate for the fact that the ball is not at chest height but lying on the ground. If you stand erect and make a few baseball swings with a club, then tilt forward in position for a golf swing and swing with the same feeling as in the baseball swing, you will appreciate what we mean by the "horizontal" working of the body.

The Role of the Body

Now let's consider how the body times the swing. We've established that the arms do the swinging part of the golf swing. In contrast, the body turns and the body coils and recoils. *The body does not swing. It reacts to the swing.* The body adds to the width of the arm swing, it adds to the length of the arm swing, and it times the swing. And it does this by what we call the "Proper Order of Movement" in the swing.

When you swing your arms back the first reaction will occur in the shoulders; the shoulders will start to coil. The shoulders in turn will coil the torso, the torso will coil the hips, the hips will pull the left side around—and the left thigh and the left knee, depending on how long a swing you're making. The right leg is also wound up by the action of the hips. All these actions are a sequential reaction to the arm swing. Now, in starting down, you must use the same principle: *The first move is with the arms.* Regardless of what type of swing you're trying to make, the first move must be the downward swing of the arms, because it's the only way you can put the club into the right downswing path to meet the ball squarely at impact.

There are two paths to the swing? You're darned right there are. The downswing path, when you view the player from the front, will be "inside" that of the backswing. This is because in the downswing you are letting the lower body release. The arms will start the downward swing, but the lower body release will make the downward path of the arms, hands, and club "inside" the backswing path.

In order to time the swing properly, you release from the bottom up. The left side and left leg were coiled in the backswing, and the first movement in the body is the left heel returning to the ground and the left knee moving left. Then the right side releases, again from the bottom up. The tension built up on the inside of the right thigh muscles by the coil is released sequentially. The right knee releases the right hip, which will keep the uncoiling of the shoulders until last. And between the uncoiling of the shoulders and the arm swing you can time the club into the ball perfectly so that at impact the shoulders are aligned the same way as at address—and you get a square, solid contact.

The key "feel" for the average player for the backswing is to feel width. On the downswing, the key feel is to keep the downswing path "inside" that of the backswing. And it's the blending of the arm swing with the body action that makes that possible.

Thus, the two most important questions you have to get straight in your mind are how to start the swing away from the ball and how to start the club back through the ball. The answer in both instances is the same: *The arms lead.* Then, in order to time the swing, *the body is the timer.* If you take a full turn, this gives you plenty of room and time to get the blade into a square position at the ball. You coil the body on the backswing, and you uncoil and release the right side in the downswing. This is what times the blade into the ball. If you understand these two principles, you are well on your way to understanding the true swing.

However, before we can teach the swing, you've got to learn the correct hold on the club and the right way to stand to a golf ball. If you learn that, you make it possible to acquire a good golf swing. If you don't, you will never reach your potential whatever natural talent you may have for the game.

Did you know that we, or any competent teacher, can tell within half-a-dozen strokes the handicap of a player before he ever draws the club back? Yes, there's that much difference in the way the various classes of golfer will hold the club and stand to the ball!

Our first objective, therefore, will be to teach the correct hold on the club and the correct set. Then we're going to work with you in every conceivable way so that you can learn the true swing. With a good swing in your bag, you can always enjoy your golf. Without one, you will be forever claiming you are out for the exercise.

Obitz and Farley Say:

1. The principle of "coil/recoil" is what blends the backswing and downswing into one continuous movement.

2. To learn a good golf swing, you should start with small swings. You should learn quarter-swings with the 7-iron and then progress through the half- and three-quarter swings to the full swing. Attempting to learn the full swing with a wooden club first has doomed many golfers to being poor players all their lives.

3. The golf swing is composed of two working parts. The arms create the swing, leading both backswing and downswing, and the body times the swing by means of the coil/recoil action. It's the blending of the arm swing and body action that makes a fine swing.

3

How You Stand Is How You Swing: The Hold

THERE'S NO GREAT SECRET to telling a player's calibre from the way he takes his grip and address position. To the experienced eye, it's quite obvious that the good player is doing far more than merely getting into position to stand at the ball. He's assuming the grip that is right for the swing he is about to make, he is aligning his body to the target, he is setting up controls in his body that will establish both coil/recoil and swinging action, and he is preparing not just for a backswing, but a free swing through the ball. He is sensing all these things while his mind is focused on the desired trajectory of the shot to the target. If you know what to look for—and by the end of the next chapter you will know what points to look for—it is not difficult.

In contrast, the poor player gropes for some way to make the grip feel comfortable, forever adjusting his distance from the ball, manipulating his body into artificial positions, or just standing up to the ball any old way. His mind is rather obviously on the way he will take the club *back* rather than the way he will move *through the ball*, and it's apparent that, while he is looking at the target, he does not "see" it in the golfing sense as the objective that shapes everything he is doing. Above all else, he has no system.

There are all sorts of nuances that identify the class of golfer in front of us. A tightness in the waggle, for example, could immediately

17

signal us that the player lacks free wrist work. Even if everything else in the address were more or less correct, this would automatically indicate a 10–14 handicapper.

With a good golfer, everything needed for a good golf swing is, so to speak, "built in." With a middle handicapper, some of the needed building blocks are missing. With the poor golfer, nothing is built in and the seeds of bad swings are quite apparent.

One thing we'll promise you: If you learn how to stand up to the ball like a pro and nothing else, your chances of making a good swing and consequently producing a good shot will increase 100 percent. If you don't learn it, whatever success you have at golf will be inconsistent —here today and gone tomorrow.

The Correct Hold on the Club

Until now we have used the word "grip" to describe the way a player should hold the club because it is the word commonly in use. However, if we had you on the lesson tee, you would never hear us use it. Instead, we talk about the correct "hold" on the club. We will use the word "hold" in this sense throughout the remainder of this book (and the word "grip" solely to indicate the handle of the club).

Our insistence on the word "hold" is no mere semantic hair-splitting. In our opinion, the word "grip" has prevented many people from ever swinging a club correctly because to most people "grip" suggests *grip tightly*. They have the idea that they have to put a "death" grip on the club so that it does not turn in the hands during the swing. As you will see, this is not necessary.

For now, we'll say this: A tight "grip" will kill a swinging action faster than just about anything else. Why? Because it tightens up the wrists and forearms so much that they cannot function as they should. Instead of a free swinging motion, all you can make is a type of punch shot using the big muscles of the upper arms and shoulders. (The "punch shot" *is* in our vocabulary, but a punch shot comes under shot-making, which is a variation on the regular swing.) You should swing the club freely on all shots except where a special shot is required—and even then the variation from the regular swing is quite slight, certainly not as much as would be induced by a "death" grip on the club. So much for the word "grip."

In the correct hold on the club, the hands must be placed on the club so that they can function as a unit during the swing. In the golf swing the hands do not function independently. One of the problems of

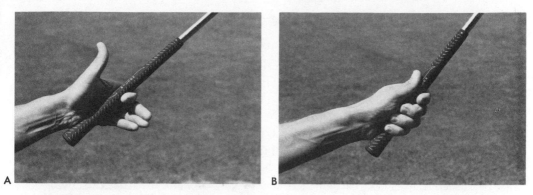

To assume correct left-hand hold, cradle the club in the middle joint of the forefinger and under the butt of the hand (A). Close the fingers and lower the thumb so that it lies just to the right of center on the grip (B).

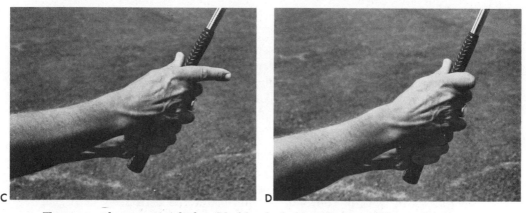

To assume the correct right-hand hold, take hold with the middle two fingers with the index finger pointed directly away from you. Slide the right hand up the grip until the third finger of the right hand meets the left forefinger, and the lifeline of the right hand fits over the left thumb (C). Complete the hold by wrapping the little finger around the knuckle of the left forefinger, and lower the right thumb to the grip just to the left of center. Your hold should now resemble photo D.

golf, in fact, is that we're so used to using our hands in very active ways—hammering a nail, writing our name, opening a door, or whatever. In golf, the hands are along for a free ride, so to speak, given them by the action in the forearms through flexible wrists. They follow; they don't initiate. Basically, all the hands do is to hold the club in position during the swing.

The feeling in the hands, once the correct hold is taken, should be that, if someone were to pour water over the hands and the water were then flash frozen, nothing in the swing could crack that layer of ice.

Let's put it another way: The correct hold on the club must be such as to discourage lifting, pushing, or any independent action that would pull the hands apart or permit them to relax their hold and alter the position of the clubface through twisting or turning of the club. It should encourage the hands to be swung as a living part of the club.

In taking the hold, we think a very simple way for the beginner to do it is to stand erect, hold the club lightly in the left hand, and sole the club naturally by your left side. Now relax the hold of the left hand a second to check that your left arm is hanging naturally from the shoulder and that you have made no artificial effort to turn the arm either to the right or left. Once you're satisfied the arm is hanging freely, position the grip of the club in the left forefinger so that the grip is cradled in the middle joint. Now press down on the top of the grip so that you're holding the club between the forefinger and a point just under the butt of the hand.

To test whether the hold is secure, attempt to lift the club. If the club slips off the butt of the hand, then you didn't get enough of the butt of the hand over the grip. Adjust until you can lift and re-sole the club several times without any slippage. Then close the fingers of the left hand on the grip and lower the thumb on the grip directly downwards so that it lies just to the right of center on the grip. Your hands will then have completed the left hand hold (see illustration, page 19).

Overlapping Hold. To assume the right hand hold, bring the club forward in front of you. Lay the grip across the bottom joints of the middle two fingers just below the palm. Take hold of the club with the middle two fingers only in such a way that the index finger points directly away from you. Now slide the right hand up the grip until the third finger of the right hand meets the forefinger of the left and the lifeline on the right hand fits squarely over the left thumb. To complete the hold, the little finger should wrap around the knuckle of the left forefinger, the right forefinger take hold of the grip, and the right thumb be lowered to the grip just to the left of center.

There are several points you should understand about the principles behind the hold you've just taken. They're important because no such thing as "the average golfer" exists; there are just "golfers," and every one of them is an individual.

The hold you assumed is called the "overlapping." Obitz and Farley recommend it because it does two things for you that are most important. First, it joins the hands together into the desired "unit." Second, most golfers, being right-handed, find that the overlapping hold equalizes the strength of the two hands by removing the little finger of

(A) Overlapping hold.   (B) Interlocking hold.   (C) 10 finger hold.

the right from the grip. We would recommend it to the vast majority of golfers.

Interlocking Hold. It's been our experience that for a few golfers the overlapping hold is unsuitable. People with short fingers sometimes find it uncomfortable. In such a case, we suggest the "interlocking" hold, in which the little finger of the right hand lies between the index finger and second finger of the left hand and the left index finger lies between the little finger and third finger of the right hand (see illustration). The interlocking hold also unifies the hands; however, it does not balance the strengths of each hand for the average right-handed golfer as well as the overlapping since the left forefinger is off the club as well as the little finger of the right hand. Many successful golfers, including Jack Nicklaus and Lloyd Mangrum, have used the interlocking grip.

10-finger Hold. For a small minority of golfers neither the overlapping hold nor the interlocking hold is satisfactory. For them the "10-finger" hold, so called because all ten fingers are on the grip, can be worth exploring. The 10-finger hold has one drawback—*it does not unify the hands* as do the other two holds. Thus the hands can function independently, leading to inconsistency. However, it has one undeniable strength: It allows the right hand to act more powerfully and it can yield slightly more distance than either the overlapping or interlocking.

It can be useful as a first grip for juniors of both sexes and for some players who lack much physical strength. However, one thing we've found in teaching is that it never pays to be too dogmatic about anything in golf. Art Wall, as fine a player as ever lived and still winning in his 50s on the PGA tour, uses the 10-finger hold. Former PGA champion Bob Rosburg also uses this grip. So if you find you can get more distance with the 10-finger without sacrificing accuracy, then we say use it.

Whether you use the overlapping, interlocking, or 10-finger is of much less importance than whether you are holding the club the right way. What we now have to say applies to all three holds.

Take hold of the club in the manner we've described and, with the sole of the club resting on the ground in front of you, straighten out the fingers of both hands. You will note that the palms of your hands are parallel to each other. This is one of the most important fundamentals of the correct hold. Unless the palms are parallel, it will be difficult for the hands to function as a unit during the swing.

To appreciate this fact for yourself, try this experiment: Hold a 7-iron as we've described and stand up and address an imaginary ball. Now just swing the club back and forth a couple of times, as if it were a pendulum on a grandfather clock. Swing the club as a unit with the arms, allowing the shoulders and wrists to move responsively to the action. *Notice that with the correct hold it's very easy to swing the club and hands as a unit.*

Now deliberately take a hold where the palms are not parallel; turn the left hand way to the left and the right hand way to the right. Now attempt to swing the club pendulum fashion. You'll immediately feel the difference. It's now very difficult to truly swing the club. The left hand wants to jerk the club up, bending the wrists much more quickly than before. And coming through the "ball," the right hand wants to jerk the club through. There's a "push-me-pull-you" action in the hands that destroys the swinging action. What you've just done is only a slight exaggeration of what many high-handicappers do when they hold the club and attempt to swing. As you can see, they have no chance!

Now try the reverse of the previous hold. Turn your left hand way to the right and the right hand as far to the left as you can in the circumstances. Again, attempt the pendulum swing. Note how the pressures build up in the hands that weren't there to start with. Note how jerky the action is. Actually, we shouldn't describe this as a "swing"; a swing is a pure action, and this is too jerky an effort to fit our definition.

Let's go back to the overlapping hold we recommended and study it further. Assume the original hold and bring the club up in front of your face. You'll probably see two to two and a half knuckles on both hands and the V's formed between the forefingers and thumbs of each hand will point more or less straight up the shaft. You are probably looking at the hold on the club that will be ideal for you all your golfing life.

Why do we say probably? Because, again, you have to allow for individual variation to some extent. Some great golfers have assumed holds on the club where the hands are turned somewhat to the left of what we've described and others a little farther to the right. Recreational golfers also have to make adjustments of this sort. This has to do with the flight pattern you achieve, whether you hit the ball straight or curve it to the left (hook) or right (slice). Basically, if you slice the ball you should move your hands to the right; if you hook the ball, you should move your hands to the left. (We'll handle these adjustments in more detail later.) Keep in mind that any adjustments you make by turning the hands to the right or left should be made with the hold being moved as one piece. In other words, both hands should be turned the same amount to the right or left, keeping the "palms-parallel" concept. Otherwise, you'll end up with a hold which is unbalanced and in which the hands will tend to function independently and not as a unit.

To make our next point, we ask you to compare three holds on the club. The first is the one we recommend, the second is the one in which the left hand is turned very much to the right and the right hand very much to the left, and the third involves taking a regular hold with the left hand and then turning the right hand very much to the right.

Besides the fact that the palms are parallel in the recommended hold but not in either of the other two, there is another important difference. In our recommended hold, the right hand fits over the left thumb like a glove. The muscle at the base of the right thumb is on the left side of the left thumb, the lifeline of the right hand is along the center of the left thumb, and the right side of the left thumb is cradled in the palm of the right hand. The hands could not be more "together" whatever you tried.

The same cannot be said of the other two holds. In the second hold, the right hand almost floats in space. In the third, there is a lot of air between the lifeline of the right palm and the left thumb. Neither hold has it all "together"; both invite movement in the hands during the swing, which obviously leads to inconsistency.

Now we would like you to study the position of the club in your hands. Let's examine the left hand hold first. Take the recommended left hand hold and open up the hand supporting the club with the right hand. You will note that the grip of the club runs diagonally across the hand from the crook of the left forefinger to under the butt of the hand. As we've seen, if the club were to lie higher in the hand there would be no support for the club, there would be no "balancing system" between the forefinger and under the butt of the hand.

However, there is another possibility: Suppose the grip of the club ran from the crook of the left forefinger below the baseline of the fingers—in other words, a hold in the fingers. If you try this finger hold, you will soon convince yourself it's as bad as the other extreme. You'll find that the only way you can complete the hold is to bring the hand down so that you can now see the whole of the back of the left hand. If you now pull on the club with the right hand, you will find that there is very little strength in the fingers; they tend to open up and loosen their hold on the grip. Again, you have the potential for inconsistency, since the pressure on the hands at the top of the swing as the club changes direction is considerable. It's certainly enough to induce the same type of loosening we've just observed. Once the club is loose in the hands, it becomes a matter of luck whether the clubface position remains the same or not. And an inconsistent clubface position means misdirected shots.

Examining the right hand hold, take the recommended hold and then try putting the grip more in the palm of the right hand. You will see that doing so forces the fingers of the right hand off the grip. If you waggle the club a few times, you will find that not only are the fingers loose on the club but the grip is sliding up and down between the forefinger and thumb. Again the unity of the correct hold is lost.

Pressure Points in the Hold

So far we've examined a correct hold on the club and the pros and cons of this hold versus other possibilities. Now we want to consider the role of the individual fingers and the desired pressure points.

The forefingers and thumbs of each hand are the "feelers" in the hold and the other fingers are the "grabbers." This means that the last three fingers of the left hand and the middle two of the right hold the club just a *little* more firmly than the forefingers and thumbs.

Why should this be so? Why shouldn't the forefingers and thumbs be the "grabbers," since we know that they're by far the most active members of the hands in most everyday activities? Well, let's do it and see what happens.

Take the recommended hold and then squeeze the forefingers and thumbs together hard. Immediately you'll find that the forearms are tight and that the wrists have lost some flexibility. This is obviously no good; we've established that in the true swing the forearms have to be free to swing the hands via the medium of flexible wrists.

Now reverse the process. Hold lightly with the forefingers and thumbs and a *little* more firmly with the last three fingers of the left hand and middle two of the right. You'll find that only the undersides of the forearms are tightened a fraction, and the wrists—test them—are free to move.

Some pressure is needed in the correct hold. Not a lot, but some. That's because the hold has to withstand the forces acting on it during the swing that would otherwise loosen even a good hold. But the only places for pressure that make sense are the last three fingers of the left hand and the middle two of the right.

How do I stop the forefingers and thumbs from grabbing? we hear you ask. That's a fair question, and our answer will take care not only of the forefingers and thumbs but also of another problem. Many golfers assume the correct hold, swing away from the ball, and, at the top of the swing, allow the palm of the right hand to come away from the left.

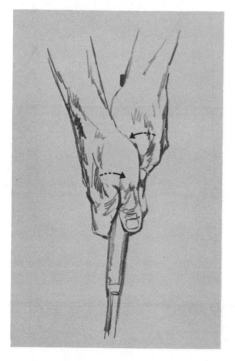

A light pressure of the left hand toward the right and the right hand toward the left firms up the "golfer's muscles" (indicated by arrows). This prevents any looseness in the hold and also prevents the forefingers and thumbs from "grabbing."

This is undesirable because the hands will instinctively attempt to close the gap on the downswing in a "grabbing" motion. This can throw the clubhead ahead of the hands; it is a subtle form of leverage. And since any form of leverage destroys the swinging action, we don't want it.

Now to the solution. After you have assumed the correct hold and firmed up the hold in the last three fingers of the left hand and the middle two of the right, exert a *little* pressure of the left hand toward the right and the right toward the left. *The pressure is similar to wringing out a washrag or towel.* When you do this, you'll notice that enough downward pressure is exerted by the lifeline of the right hand onto the left thumb so that there's no way the hands can "come apart" in the swing.

The "towel-wringing" pressure does something else for you: It firms up what Henry Cotton calls the "golfer's muscles," the muscles you use to draw the thumbs to the side of each hand. In so doing it closes any "gaps" that may exist between the thumbs and the sides of each hand (which could allow some looseness in the hold), but, more important, it also prevents the forefingers and thumbs from "grabbing."

The forefingers and thumbs do have a function. In the correct hold, the thumbs oppose the forefingers so that they can feel where the club is before and during the swing. They are, in fact, the "eyes" of the golf swing. But they should "feel" the action of the swing for you and nothing else.

OBITZ AND FARLEY SAY:

1. You hold the club—you don't grip it.
2. The correct hold makes the hands function as a unit.
3. The correct hold discourages any independent action in the hands.
4. The overlapping hold is best for the majority of golfers.
5. Palms should be parallel in the correct hold. If they're not, the hands tend to work independently and not as a unit.

4
How You Stand Is How
You Swing: The Set

Now that you have the correct hold on the club, we can advance to teaching you the correct "set," the word we like to use to describe the address position. To us the word "address" suggests rather a vague way of standing to the ball, whereas the word "set" has the quality of preparedness for the swing that we look for. You set your body in terms of alignment to make a swing that will send the ball to the target. You set your limbs in position so that they are ready to make the swing. You set your muscles so that they are ready to make the swing and the vital coil/recoil action.

From one point of view, everything possible will be built in to make a true swing. And the converse will also be true: A lot of potential faulty actions will be nipped in the bud.

What we're going to teach you here is how to stand for the mini-swing with the 7-iron, since the principles about the set you learn for the short swing will be exactly the same as for longer swings. We will resolve any minor differences as we progress.

Alignment

If you have ever watched a great player set up to the ball, you will have been impressed by the meticulous care with which he aims the clubface at the target as though he were using a gunsight and then squares his feet and body to the intended line. As you will see, this care is not misplaced.

During the golf swing, as you swing the club back on the proper path, the shoulders will turn in sympathy with the swing of the arms. The turn of the shoulders brings the clubhead inside what we call the target line—the line from the ball to the target. On the downswing, the unwinding of the shoulders will bring the clubhead back to the ball from the inside to a square position at impact and then, as the shoulders continue to unwind, the clubhead continues down the target line for a short way, then swings back inside the target line again.

For a straight shot, it is essential that imaginary lines drawn across the toes, from hip to hip, and from shoulder to shoulder should be parallel to the target line (A). If the imaginary lines are aligned to the right of parallel (B) or to the left of parallel (C), then the swing will be misdirected to the right or left of target.

A

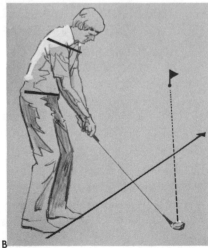

B

C

For this inside-to-square-to-inside swing through the ball to happen, it is essential that, for any straight shot, the feet, hips, and shoulders be square to the target line. By square we mean that if you were to draw imaginary lines across the toes, and from hip to hip, and from shoulder to shoulder, these lines would be parallel to the target line. If the toe, hip, and shoulder lines were aligned to the left of parallel, the swing would be misdirected to the left of the target; if the lines were aligned to the right of parallel, the swing would be misdirected to the right of the target. It's that simple.

The other two important ingredients of square alignment are the direction in which the clubface is pointing and the hold on the club. If either is not aligned properly, the shot will be misdirected.

Our experience has been that amateurs are extremely careless about clubface alignment. We find that many habitually set up to the ball with the clubface in a closed (looking left of target) or open (looking right of target) position. A high percentage of these more or less put the club down at random, trusting to instinct to produce square alignment.

Consequences of Improper Clubface Alignment

One reason for this cavalier approach may be that they've never considered the consequences of not having the clubface square. However, let us tell you that a square clubface is just as important as square body

(A) Open clubface. (B) Square clubface. (C) Closed clubface.

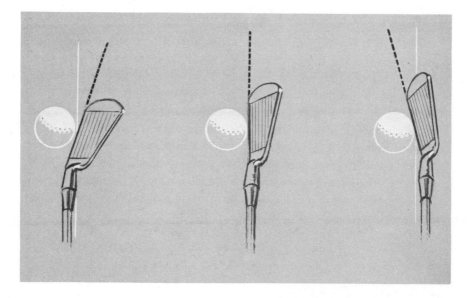

alignment. Even if your body were square and you produced the correct inside-to-square-to-inside swing path, if the clubface were closed at impact it would impart counter-clockwise spin on the ball, curving the ball to the left. If the clubface were open, it would impart clockwise spin, curving the ball to the right.

Another reason why golfers don't manage to aim the clubface correctly is that they simply don't know what part of the clubface to aim with. With woods, it is comparatively easy to line up the clubface at the target. The clubface and the face insert (if any) are normally of a different color from the paint on the rest of the clubhead—so you use the line across the top of the clubface for reference and simply put this line at right angles to the target line. On some woods the manufacturer gives a little help in alignment: Some have a T-square painted behind the center of the clubface, others have the maker's name written across the top of the wood so that it forms a rough T-square with the line across the top of the clubface. If you have these aids on your woods, use them.

With the irons the situation is a little more complex, due to the variety of models produced. If you have a fairly conventional set of irons, chances are that the leading edge (lower front edge) of the blade is straight. If it is, then this is the line you must put at right angles to the target line. If the leading edge is curved as you look down at it, which is often the case on the shorter irons (8- and 9-irons, pitching and sand wedges), then use the lowest scoring line on the clubface to line up with. The one thing you must not do is to line up using the line made by the top of the blade. If you do that, you will be closing the face so that it points left of the target. It's really surprising how many golfers make this mistake!

The hold on the club is another important factor in square alignment. In discussing the correct hold, we emphasized the importance of building a hold that would function as a unit and also encourage a swinging action rather than any form of leverage. But there's still another aspect to the hold, and that is its "squareness" in relation to the square alignment of the body and the clubface. For it makes no sense to set the clubface squarely at the target and align the body squarely to the target if the connector between the two—the hold—has the potential to upset the original squareness of the clubface during the swing. Although the hold we recommended earlier did in fact satisfy this requirement, we would like to go into this in more detail here.

Take a 7-iron and assume the hold we recommended. Stand up to an imaginary ball and make certain the clubface is square. Now open your hands. You'll note that not only are the palms parallel to each other, they are also parallel to the scoring lines on the blade. Thus everything is squared to the target—shoulders, hips, feet, hold, and clubface.

We wish we could leave the subject of alignment here, but we can't, in all honesty, do so. Many golfers who come to our schools know theoretically that everything should be squared to the target in the set, but still they manage to get it wrong. If this sounds like you, don't despair. You're not alone in finding it difficult to set up square to the target. Even professionals get into trouble on this point. But when they do, they take steps to correct the problem at their next practice session.

How to Check for Square Alignment

What you should do is to lay down one club outside the ball and direct it straight at the target, then lay down another club parallel to it just in front of where your toes will be for the club you are using. Then, when you take your set at the ball, you can check that your feet, hips, and shoulders are square with the line at your feet. If you are in fact misaligned to the left or right of target your first reaction will probably be, "But I thought I was square!" There you have it: One of the frustrating things about this game is that you can be firmly convinced that you are doing something correctly when you're not. No one can see himself or herself in action—unless you use some visual aid (of which more later).

You should periodically check your alignment, and the "two-club" method is the way to do it. Many tour players at a tournament, especially after the day's play is over, in the afternoon and evening when they are working on their game rather than warming up, will practice this way. If it's good enough for them, it's good enough for you!

When you're out on the course, you can't lay the clubs down and play the shot with them in position. (This would constitute an "artificial device," in violation of Rule 37-9a of the Rules of Golf.) But what you can do is to approach the ball in a logical, step-by-step method that will ensure square alignment.

Here we'll take a time out to describe how a typical high-handicapper approaches the ball. Having taken the club from the bag, he goes over to the ball and places his feet in position. Then perhaps he takes his hold on the club and places it behind the ball. Then he notices he's too close to the ball, so he shuffles his feet back a little way. Then he takes a look at the target and realizes that the club isn't square to the target, so he points it more to the left—or to the right, as the case may be—altering the position of the hold as he does so. Then he hits the ball.

Dozens of things can go wrong with such a haphazard method. The player's feet and body could be misaligned; his hold on the club could be moved from a square position by his last-second clubface adjustment. The chances of everything being square are poor.

In contrast, a good player has a fixed *pattern* that ensures that everything is in order—and we'll go into that pattern at the end of this chapter. Here we want to point out the main differences between the high-handicapper's approach to the ball and the good player's, as regards correct alignment.

When you placed your clubs in the "two-club" alignment test, where were you standing? Yes, you were *behind the ball*, looking at the target. This is the only position from which you can truly align those clubs. The same thing applies when setting up to a golf ball. You must start from a position behind the ball, looking down toward the target. Then you can draw an imaginary line back from the target to the ball, and this will be the line you set the clubface square to.

The high-handicapper put his feet in position before ensuring that either the clubface was square or his body was square. This will not do. The good golfer will first position himself behind the ball. Then he makes certain his hold on the club is square to the clubface while his club is resting in a square position on the ground. He moves to the ball, positioning the club square to the target line he has picked out. He then measures himself to the ball and places his feet and body parallel to the imaginary target line. He sets the clubface first, then the body—*not the other way around.*

Notice how the good golfer used the target to align himself from the beginning. The high-handicapper used it only when he was already standing up to the ball, when the changes he makes may upset square alignment—if indeed he was square at any point in the proceedings.

Here we would like to emphasize another point we think is vital to good alignment: When you square the clubface to the target line and measure yourself to the ball you should do so *with your feet together.* Many golfers step into the ball with their right foot leading—and from there put their left foot in position and then their right. But they're leaving out a vital step which, without a bit of effort, would make certain their body was square to the target line. If you place your feet together while squaring the clubface to the target line, you know at that point that a line across your toes is square to the target line. If both toes are square to the target line, your hips and shoulders are square also. It is then a very simple matter to move your left foot a little to the left and your right foot a little to the right, maintaining this square relationship. Many fine golfers have made "feet together" a part of their set-up pattern. Among the old-timers, Lloyd Mangrum made quite a fetish of this; today Johnny Miller has thought it worthwhile to make a habit of it.

When you stand with your feet together preparatory to moving the left foot and right foot into position, you should use everything at your command to ensure square alignment. This includes your imagination. A mental image we have found very useful is one we call "driving the highway."

Imagine a four-lane highway with a divider in the middle stretching straight away from you. The target lies on the divider close to you (or in the distance for longer shots). When you step up to the ball you square the clubface to the line of the divider and square your toes to the left-hand edge of the road, looking down it if you're a right-hander or to the right-hand side if you're a left-hander. Spread your feet apart, keeping your toes lined up with the edge of the road, and everything is square as it should be.

Another aid to good alignment is "spot" golf. We've left it until last because, frankly, it doesn't suit everybody. From behind the ball, you pick a spot just in front of the ball on line to the target. Then, to square the clubface to the target, you square it to a line from the spot back to the ball, rather than from the target to the ball. As Jack Nicklaus, who uses this method, says, it's easier to line up from a spot a couple of feet in front of the ball than from a target that may be over 200 yards away. This, theoretically, is true. However, some golfers find that when they get over the ball the spot they picked out from behind the ball no longer looks as though it's on line to the target. This can breed anxiety which, by itself, can wreck the swing. If you like the "spot" and find it useful, then use it. If you're not comfortable using the "spot," then line up at the target itself and use the whole target line for reference.

Getting Set for the Mini-swing

With what you've learned so far, you can take the correct hold on the club, identify the target line from behind the ball, and set the clubface squarely behind the ball on line to the target from the feet-together position. Now let's help you complete your set in preparation for the "mini-swing."

Your first move would be to take the correct hold at the lower end of the grip. Why? Because it cuts down on the width of the arc and gives you more control. Then you would move the left foot a couple of inches or so to the left and the right foot a slightly longer distance to the right, maintaining the square alignment of the toes parallel to the target line. Why such a narrow stance? Remember that we're going to start with a "mini-swing," a few feet back and a few feet through. You don't need the wide stance necessary for the longer swing you would make with a distance club such as a driver. (A long swing generates a lot of centrifugal force and for that you need a wider base. Here we are talking about a finesse shot of no more than 15 yards or so.)

Now to the position of the feet: We ask you to stand in such a way that your right foot is at a right angle to the target line and your left foot is turned outwards a little to the left. The reason is that the turn of the hips is controlled by the position in which you place your feet.

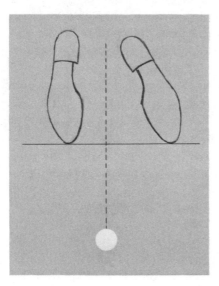

As a general rule, the right foot should be placed at right angles to the target line; the left foot should be turned outwards a little to the left.

If you experiment a little with various placements of the feet, you can readily demonstrate this to yourself. The more you turn the right foot to the right, the easier it is to turn the hips fully to the right and the harder it is to turn them to the left. On the other hand, the more you toe in the right foot to the left, the more difficult it is to turn your hips to the right and the easier it is to turn them to the left. The left foot works in exactly the opposite way: left foot toed in to the right, easy hip turn to the right, difficult turn to the left; left foot toed out, harder to turn to the right, easier to turn to the left.

The foot position we recommend you start with is actually the best compromise that permits a free swing and the correct coil/recoil action. With the right foot at right angles to the target line, the hip turn will be restricted enough to create torsion between the turn of the shoulders and the turn of the hips. The left foot being toed out slightly restricts the hip turn going back and assists the coil. And the left foot being turned out a little definitely assists the recoil action of the downswing, while the placement of the right foot sets the right leg in good position for the release.

There is one important aspect of this foot position we think you should be aware of. You started with the feet together, with the ball on a line directly between your feet. Your balance at that point was evenly distributed between your feet. You then moved your left foot a few

To set up with the correct posture, first stand up naturally, just as if you were having a conversation (A). Then tilt forward from the hips, counterbalancing yourself by allowing the seat to be pushed back slightly (B).

inches to the left and your right foot slightly farther to the right, maintaining the square alignment. Moving the right foot away from the target a little farther than the left is done with the thought that the right foot will have to bear the burden of the weight on the backswing, and so you set it in position where it can do this easily. The distribution of weight between the feet is still even, yet more of the body weight is behind the ball, which facilitates the backswing motion. The left foot is placed ahead of the ball so that when you swing through the ball the left foot can take the weight at the finish.

The overall posture of the body should be very natural. We like to ask initially that you just stand naturally, as if you were having a conversation. There should be enough bend in your knees so that the knees are unlocked. Your head should be set upright on the neck in a comfortable position. Now, simply tilt forward from the hips without disturbing the set of the spine or the neck. As you tilt forward with the upper body, counterbalance yourself by allowing your seat to be pushed back slightly. This enables you to keep your back in the desired straight position and to retain the balance midway between the balls of your feet and the heels. (Note: You never want any weight on the toes.) You should allow your arms to hang naturally from your shoulders; they shouldn't be pushed out away from nor in close to the body. As a rough guide, there should be at least a hand's width between the club and the thigh.

Now let's examine the position of the shoulders and how it affects the set of the arms. The ideal position would find you with the left shoulder a little higher than the right, the left arm extended straight, but comfortably straight, and the right arm more relaxed than the left with the right elbow more in toward the body than the left. If you watched a good golfer setting up to the ball from behind (looking toward the target), you'd see that the right arm would be "inside" the left. You would also find that although the right shoulder was lower than the left the square shoulder alignment was maintained.

This set of the arms and shoulders prepares for several important functions during the swing. The square alignment of the shoulders, as you know, prepares for the correct inside-to-square-to-inside swing. The extended position of the left arm is vital because the left arm is responsible for creating the arc of the swing: If it's not essentially straight at the start, then obviously the arc of the swing will not be constant. The right arm must be more relaxed and "in" toward the side so that it can fold naturally on the backswing. We say "naturally" because the action of the right arm in the golf swing is as natural as winding up to throw a ball underhand. And the action in the left arm is as natural as that for the right: Essentially, the left arm action is the same as the backhand for the southpaw tennis player.

Shoulders Should Not Be Level

Having said all that, we have to point out that this set of the arms and shoulders is an area in which many beginners—and many experienced golfers—go wrong. And the reason they go wrong is that they try to keep the shoulders level as they set up. They don't appreciate the fact that the left shoulder must be up and the right shoulder down to accommodate for the right hand being lower than the left on the grip. This basic misunderstanding leads to two other setups quite different from the one we've just described—and both of them are wrong!

In the first one, the golfer tries to compensate for the lower hold of the right hand by allowing his left arm to bend and straightening his right arm. He maintains the square alignment of the shoulders, but what he is doing is diametrically opposed to the correct set. When he does this, the club is invariably forced outside the target line on the backswing because the right elbow does not have a chance to fold properly going back. The left arm, meanwhile, is put in such a weak position that it cannot fulfill its function of creating the arc of the swing. Instead, it goes along for the ride dominated by the right arm. In the downswing, the golfer will make an outside-in attack on the ball.

The second faulty setup often leads from the first. Perhaps the golfer stands up in the fashion just described and someone tells him, "Your left arm has got to be straight." He then tries to straighten the left arm while still holding the right arm straight. The result forces the shoulders into an open alignment: The left shoulder is forced back so that the shoulders are now aligned way to the left of the square position. The golfer's state is now worse than it was at first—he will swing outside the target line worse than ever going back, and the resulting out-to-in path through the ball has to lead to a slice.

Another aspect of the shoulder-arm relationship in the set is that you're also striving for the proper impact position. At impact the club should be an extension of the left arm. That is, if you view the player from the front at impact, there should be a straight line from the left shoulder down the left arm and clubshaft. It also means that the back of the left wrist should be in line with the left side of the forearm. If anything, the back of the left wrist should be in advance of (closer to) the target than the back of the left hand and therefore the clubhead. What controls this is the position of the left shoulder at impact: The shoulder should be as high at impact as in the set. The high left shoulder is what keeps the back of the left wrist leading toward the target. If you drop the left shoulder in the set (shoulders too level), you'll not make a good swing because you'll tend to have the hands too far back in the stance to the right, and when you do this you break the left wrist—there's a large concave curve from the back of the left hand in to the back of the left wrist and out again to the left forearm. Swing from this position—where the clubhead is ahead of the hands—and the clubhead will be ahead of the hands at impact; you'll be flipping the hands or scooping the ball.

Basically, you should set up to the ball with more or less a straight line down the left arm and shaft (A), although a little break in the left wrist is permissible. During the swing, the force created will result in the left arm and shaft being in line or with the back of the left wrist being a little in front of the left hand (B).

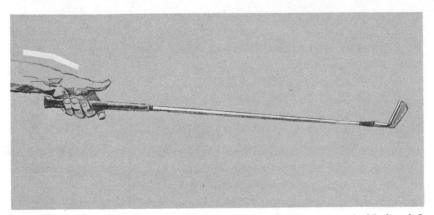

To get the feel of the correct "arched" position of the wrists, hold the club in the back three fingers of your left hand at shoulder height. Complete the hold with the right hand and the wrists will be correctly arched.

Basically, you should set up with more or less a straight line down the left arm and shaft to achieve the desired impact position. However, the exact position does depend on your build—more precisely, on the width of your shoulders. For a broad-shouldered person to have the shaft and left arm in line, he would have to play the ball too far forward. So it's permissible for him to have a little break in the left wrist. The narrower your shoulders, the nearer you can get to the straight line setup. In the swing, the forearms swing the hands and lead the wrists, hands, and club into the ball; and this is why you can still achieve the correct impact position, with the left arm in line with the shaft, whatever the exact position you have to adopt in the set.

If you viewed a good player from the side, you would see that his wrists were slightly "arched." To get the feel of this, take a club in your left hand only. Bring the club up to shoulder height and point it away from you so that there is pretty much a straight line horizontally down the left arm and club shaft. If you hold the club with just the back three fingers—that is, take the forefinger and thumb off the grip—you'll see that the club is a perfect extension of the left arm and that your left wrist is in the correct "slightly arched" position. Now complete the hold with the right hand and tilt forward into the set—you are in perfect position!

What makes this exercise work is holding the club in the last three fingers of the left hand. If you relaxed the hold with those fingers you would be "over-arched," and if you held with the forefinger and thumb you would have dropped the hands too much when set at the ball.

Beginners should practice this drill until the correct set of the wrists is a habit. More experienced golfers should use it from time to time to check that their wrists are in fact in good position.

"Left Arm Set" and "Leg Set"

Before we conclude this description of the correct set, we need to make two other essential points. We've left them till last because in practice you make these little adjustments as the final moves before waggling and going into the swing. We call them the "left arm set" and the "leg set."

The "left arm set" is your guarantee that the shoulders will respond to the swing of the arms. If you just let both arms hang limply from the shoulders the shoulders will probably lag behind as the forearms swing the club away—or worse, the shoulders will turn hardly at all. So you position the inside of the upper left arm lightly against the left pectoral muscle in the chest. In this way, you activate and firm up slightly not only the upper left arm but also the whole left shoulder area, which includes the big muscle below the shoulder in the back. Now, when the forearms swing the club back, the shoulders will turn automatically with them.

In the "leg set" you just set the knees a little inward toward each other, the right knee a little more than the left. This position of the legs retains even distribution of the weight between the feet while placing the weight on the inside of the feet. In this way you activate the inside muscles of the legs, encourage a stable platform for the swing, and inhibit lateral movements of the body to the right or left. Such swaying movements during the swing make accurate contact with the ball a matter of chance because, in effect, you are allowing the center of the swing to drift back and forth.

The inward set of the legs also encourages proper leg movement during the swing. On the backswing, the left leg should break toward the ball as the hip turn progresses. Setting the left leg inward makes it easy for the left leg to accomplish this simply as a reaction to the swing. The inward set of the right leg sets up proper coiling action in the right leg on the backswing. As the backswing progresses, the muscles on the inside of the right thigh become progressively more taut until they are, so to speak, forced to recoil in the downswing.

Many people think that setting up to the ball correctly is done to accommodate the backswing alone. The set does set up the backswing, but it's much more important than that. You set yourself comfortably at the ball with the thought that you are going to make a *complete swing*—back and through—and that you'll just catch the ball as part of the swing. Thus the set has to be a position in which it is comfortable to make the backswing, comfortable to catch the ball at impact, and comfortable to swing through the ball into a complete finish without interference. You're not going to make a direct hit at the ball—that leads to chopping.

The Waggle and the Forward Press

Now that you have the correct set, we recommend that you take a "waggle." This is simply a small movement of the club away from the ball and then back to the ball, a movement which can be made once or several times, at your option. In effect, it's a mini-start to the swing; although primarily done by the arms working the hands and wrists back and forth, the body can give a little to the motion as long as the framework of the set is preserved. The purpose of the waggle is to free you from any excess tension that may have crept in while you were assuming the set.

While waggling, you are previewing in your mind the shot you are about to make. For this reason, there is no one waggle for every shot. For the mini-swing we are going to start you off with, a waggle carrying the club back a few inches may well be enough. For a longer swing, the waggle could carry the club back a couple of feet.

Remember that during the swing the forearms swing the hands (and with them the club) via the medium of flexible wrists. So while you are waggling you should also check that the wrists are free, the hands ready to be swung, and the forearms activated for their role in initiating the swing.

After your last waggle, you set the club behind the ball. It is then important to make a slight forward press. It's difficult—if not impossible—to begin the swing from a standing start, and therefore every good player makes a slight motion toward the target prior to swinging the club away into the backswing. One can't be too dogmatic about the precise method used to make the forward press; it can be done with the knees, the feet, the hands, or any combination of these. The only objective is to allow the swing to start smoothly as a recoil from the slight motion forward.

However, there is one element we would like you to include in your forward press, whatever its final form. That is the "towel-wring-ing" pressure of one hand toward the other that we described in the action on the correct hold. Not only does it physically "unitize" the grip, but it also serves to remind you that the hands are about to be swung as a unit with no independent action of the hands. It's a last-second reminder that you're about to *swing* the hands and the club, not push them, pick them up, or twist them in either direction.

The Countdown Pattern

We said earlier in this chapter that every good golfer has a fixed pattern for taking the set. Not only does this add orderliness to the whole proceeding, it serves as a mental checklist that everything is proceeding according to plan and that nothing has been forgotten to ensure the success of the shot. It's like a NASA countdown: At each stage various systems are checked out, and only if they do in fact check out can the countdown proceed.

We urge you to make the "countdown" pattern we are about to suggest a habit. It incorporates all the elements of the correct set we've been discussing and literally makes for "fail-safe" operation during the swing. Another intangible benefit is that it builds up your confidence step by step as it keeps your mind focused on the shot at hand.

There's only one element we've left out of the countdown, and that is the number of "looks" you make at the target after you step in toward the ball. This aspect is so personal that it defies any fixed prescription—yet it is a vital difference between a good player and an indifferent one. Just about everything a good player does while taking the set is done with reference to the target or while taking "looks" at the target. And they can occur from the moment you step in to the ball right up to the last waggle. What we're saying is: Feel free to let these "looks" occur naturally—but don't leave them out!

One final point about our recommended countdown: You shouldn't see it as the only way to do it—or believe that every item must come in precisely this order. There's leeway in golf for individual-ity, and every golfer should adapt and modify our pattern to suit his tastes. Feel free to reshuffle these elements, but don't leave any one of them out. Make them a habit and you're well on your way to a good swing—and good golf.

The Obitz-Farley Countdown Pattern

10. From behind the ball, looking at the target, adopt a square hold on the grip. Form a clear image of the swing you are about to make. See the desired trajectory of the ball to the target.

9. Step in and measure yourself to the ball with slightly arched wrists and feet together, aligning the clubface with the target.

8. Move left foot toward target, maintaining alignment on the "highway" principle.

7. Move right foot away from target, again maintaining alignment.

6. Adopt correct posture—knees slightly bent, proper tilt of body toward ball, weight counterbalanced in shoulder area with pushout of the seat to maintain straight back, arms hanging naturally from shoulders.

5. Left shoulder up, right down, shoulder alignment maintained.

4. Left arm extended, right arm soft and in to side. Right arm "inside" left.

3. Set left arm; set legs.

2. Waggle. Last time to visualize swing and desired trajectory.

1. Forward press.

0. *Swing!*

Place your feet together while squaring the clubface and the toes to the target line (A). Move your left foot a little to the left (B) and then your right foot a farther distance to the right (C), and it is very easy to maintain the desired square alignment of feet, hips and shoulders. The "feet together" move should be part of every good "countdown" pattern.

A   B   C

5

Learning the True Swing

Now THAT WE HAVE LEARNED how to stand to the ball, we may devote this chapter entirely to developing a true swing. We will begin with a "mini-swing," in effect a quarter-swing, then advance to the half, the three-quarter, and the full swing. And we'll do this progressive buildup to the full swing with a 7-iron. From there we'll go on to full swings with the 5- and 3-irons and up the fairway woods to the driver. Along the way we're going to use every means we know to give you the feel of a swinging action: You will learn to tell by yourself whether your action is a swing or not, and you will learn every aspect of "swing" at our command.

We think it important for you to realize that *no effort you make to learn and understand a true swinging action is going to be wasted.* Why? Because whether you have a true swinging action or not is really what decides your potential as a golfer.

You can easily verify this by two checks. Stand at the first tee of any course at the weekend and just observe the golfers for half an hour or so. That guy who's heaving and jerking and swaying at the ball—yes, he's a 36-handicapper. That fellow who's got a nice compact action but appears a trifle stiff—he's a 10-handicap. And that man with the graceful, rhythmical action which somehow puts the most sound (and distance) on the ball—he's scratch, or maybe now a 3-handicap because he doesn't play as much as he did when he was younger.

Make the same type of observation at a tour tournament when you get the chance. Stand either at the first tee or at one end of the practice ground so that you can look down a row of golfers. You will find that, after a while, you can pick out the winners from the rabbits by the quality of their swings, by the extent that their golf actions approach perfection—the true swinging action. You'll discover that the fine swings just snap out of the total picture; you'll find yourself picking out such winners as Jack Nicklaus, Johnny Miller, Bruce Crampton, Al Geiberger, Tom Weiskopf, Art Wall, and Don January. You'll find yourself appreciating such fine swings as those of Sam Snead, Julius Boros, and Gene Littler. All of them may not be winning right now, but we'll bet you'd rather own their golf swings for an afternoon than those of three-quarters of the other golfers at the tournament.

Another, more subtle moral will emerge from your studies: If you want to play good golf all your life, you had better get yourself a true swinging action to begin with. Because you'll also see golfers out there who got away with some form of leverage or non-swinging action while they were in their prime, and now, in middle age, it's catching up with them. You'll realize how worthwhile it is to acquire a true swing so that, whatever your age, you will always have the pleasure of playing fine golf shots even if you can't score as well as you might if you devoted more time to the game. You'll know, too, that you have the potential to play good golf any time you really want to work at it. Most golfers can't make that claim.

Learning the Mini-swing

We want you to begin by making some "dry runs" without a ball. In this way you can concentrate on producing a swinging action without the added complication initially of having the ball there. The ball's important, don't get us wrong; once you have a true swinging action, watching the ball intently can and does occupy the conscious mind enough so that the subsconscious can reproduce a true swinging motion without distraction. But first you need a swinging action in the subconscious, and what we have found is that beginners and bad golfers generally concentrate so much of their effort on hitting the ball that they often become "ball bound."

To see some people hit a golf ball you would think that the ball offered the same type of resistance one encounters in chopping down a tree. (These golfers are indeed more woodsmen than swingers.) Even

Above, in the mini-swing or quarter-swing, you swing the 7-iron back to a point where the hands are just past your right leg, and then through to where your hands swing just past your left leg. Below, in the "brushing" exercise, you brush the grass for about six inches swinging back and again brush the grass for about six inches swinging through. This teaches you the correct swinging action.

this mini-swing we're about to do will send the ball on its way without much fuss. You don't have to hit *at* the ball, nor should you; you swing back and swing *through* the ball, and the ball is just swept along with the swing. We like to explain it this way: If a wrecker's ball can be swung back and then swung through, right *through* the wall to be knocked down, you aren't going to find much resistance from a little ball weighing only 1.62 ounces when you're swinging an implement weighing eight times as much.

The mini-swing (or quarter-swing) consists of swinging the 7-iron back to a point where the hands swing just past your right leg and then through to where your hands swing just past your left leg. Set up as we've recommended and swing the hands and club back with the forearms. Then swing through, allowing the recoil action to time the blade through the imaginary impact area.

The Brushing Exercise

Now if that action felt a little awkward or jerky and you suspect you lifted the club going back, or you hit the ground heavily coming through, don't despair. We have just the remedy for you. As you swing back this time, attempt to brush the top of the grass with the sole of the club for about six inches before it comes free of the grass, and, as you swing through, again brush the grass for about six inches. Try this "brushing" exercise a few times; you'll be pleasantly surprised how much smoother the whole action is and how much more of a swinging action you're achieving.

We, however, aren't surprised how this has helped you. Harry Obitz picked up "brushing" when working for Mac Smith as a lad and has treasured it ever since. He now describes in more detail the background of brushing, the proper technique to use, and what it does for you.

Harry Obitz: Back in 1922, when I was 9 years old, I started shagging balls for Mac Smith, who was then the professional at the Marin Golf and Country Club in Northern California. Mac was originally from Scotland, as were most of the pros in those days, and he possessed as fine a swing as you would want to see. Mac also taught the true swinging action, although he was not a man who talked a lot; he just *showed* you what to do.

One thing that lives in my memory is the way Mac would make a point of demonstrating the swing to his pupils before he did anything else. In those days people drank a lot of champagne, and Mac used to ask the bartender at the club to save the champagne corks for him. Now when he went out to give a lesson he would always wear a jacket and one of the pockets was full of champagne corks. He would toss the corks down on the grass at random and then he would show the pupil how he could pick the corks off the grass with the swing. Or he would throw them down in a bunker by a green and he would then pick them out of the trap with the swing. After hitting a few, he would say, "If I want the cork to fly a little farther, I just take the club back a little quicker and farther." And each time he swung, the corks would go a little farther, until he had a string of corks out there on the green for about 20 yards.

This was a wonderful way of getting the pupil's attention, I remember! It impressed on them immediately—and on me—that the swing was the thing. Wherever he hit the cork, it would go off like a bullet, with the foil end leading.

Anyway, now the pupil was eager to learn the true swing. The first thing that Mac would have him or her do, after getting the hold and set right, was to make them take at least 20 quarter-swings just brushing the grass. He made everybody do that before he would ever let them hit a ball or even let them talk! After that, he would put a ball down, and doggone it if the ball didn't go out there straight. It would go only 10 or 15 yards because it was a short swing, but even beginners could hit a nice straight little shot *provided* they brushed the grass both ways.

As for the technique of "brushing," about all Mac ever added to the basic "brush back, brush forward" thought was a dour, "Don't lean on it!" And by this he meant that if you want to acquire a true swing, you mustn't push the club down into the dirt when setting up to the ball. You must set the club *in* the grass.

The importance of the correct setting of the club behind the ball became very apparent to me when I first started teaching. I found that practically all the people coming to me for lessons had the idea that you had to push the club down onto the ground behind the ball. The set and the golf action (it certainly could not be called a true swing!) that resulted from this looked different to me, and wrong, and I wanted to find out what was different and why. Up to that point, of course, I had imitated Mac, as young people will, and just set the blade in the grass. Thanks to that and the brushing technique, I had acquired a pretty good swing.

After some experimentation, I found that if weight is put on the club, forcing it into the ground as though you were trying to poke a post into the ground, then your muscles are tense. To start the club, you have to lift the club up to relax them, and you're off to the wrong start! You're not swinging the club—you may be lifting or jerking the club with your hands, or with the hands and arms, or with the shoulders, or with a little of each. You're using *leverage* to move the club. And if you start with leverage, it's practically impossible to make the club swing later!

However, if you're setting the club *in* the grass, your muscle set is entirely different. If the fairway were, say, half an inch long, the club would be a quarter of an inch into the grass. When the club is "hanging," then you're in an ideal position to start a swinging motion.

First, you're aware of the weight of the club in your hands. You sense the weight and the necessity of starting the swing smoothly and gradually.

Then, in swinging back, you don't have to lift the club. Your shoulders are already "up"—a requisite of good swinging—and you can swing the arms, hands, and club back together. I don't say it's impossible to use leverage from the "hanging" position, but if you know the action you want, a swinging motion, the "hanging" position best prepares you to do just that.

All the best players use the "hanging" position, you know. Because of his swinging ability, I've watched Jack Nicklaus practice and play in every U.S. Open he's appeared in. And I've always noticed that he postures himself in balance in the set—he never "leans" on the club. He even practices sometimes with the club well above the grass. Go and watch him for yourself —you'll see what I mean.

Now look at the advantages of the brushing technique itself: If you're brushing the club back and through, you can't be lifting the club or beating down on the ball. Nor can you be lifting the body going back or ducking it down coming through. You've just got to swing!

Another plus of brushing is that this learning technique trains the body to follow the swing. You can't brush the grass correctly unless the body follows the arm swing. If you just use your arms going back without allowing the shoulders and legs to respond to the swinging motion, *the club will come up off the grass immediately*. If you brush correctly, the club will come up *gradually* in the backswing and be clear of the grass some six inches or so behind the ball. It's the same thing coming through the ball. If you just use your arms, you will hit down in back of the ball. But the thought of "brushing" makes you coordinate the body with the arm swing and time the blade into and through the ball, the blade then entering the grass just in back of the ball and just shaving the grass for four or five inches after the ball is hit.

Another point about brushing and what it does for you is that you have to explain to a lot of pupils—even to some advanced players—that the club has a built-in angle on the clubface, the "loft" on the club, which provides the trajectory to the ball. Before I put the ball down for them, I set a ball against the clubface and show them that the club slides under the ball through the shot and the ball climbs up on the clubface, which gives you the backspin that you want: The loft on the club sends the ball off on the right trajectory. Now all they have to do is brush back and brush through and the club will do the rest in providing the backspin and trajectory they want. The brushing technique teaches you that the angle at which you bring the club into the ball is all-important. In brushing, the club comes in from *behind* the ball and you hit the ball "away" from you. You don't have to pick the club up and chop down on the ball to get the ball up in the air. Nor do you have to "help" the ball up by scooping at it. You just brush back and brush through, and the club does it for you. You learn to trust the loft on the clubface to do its job. Once you understand that, you're on your way to being a golfer.

When I see players beating down on the ball and taking out soup-plate divots, I have to smile. It's totally unnecessary to take a big divot unless you're in a really bad lie. Mac was a man who could take anything from a niblick to a driver and hit the ball off the ground without ever scarring the turf. You could always tell where Mac had been practicing. There were no holes in the ground; the grass was just a little brown, under the big eucalyptus tree where we practiced, from his just shaving the grass. He would also practice from the bare ground. With the true swing, I've found that I never mind a bare lie; you can just pick the ball right off. You can't do that with leverage—you'll bang down and break your left hand!

The "bare lie" aspect of the thing is interesting because, when I met Dick Farley, he had a beautiful swing, yet I knew that, up to a point, he had never heard of brushing. Dick explained that he grew up in Alameda, California, playing a public course where there was no grass to speak of. *So he had to shave the grass.* He couldn't use leverage to move the club; he had to swing.

If you learn the brushing technique, you have in fact learned the heart of the golf swing. It was the first thing I learned about the swing, and probably the best thing I learned about the swing.

Now that you have a thorough understanding of how to set the club *in* the grass rather than into the ground, and of the club "hanging" rather than being pushed downward, try some more mini-swings, employing the brushing technique. The more you do this, the more you'll appreciate that "brushing" gives you the feel of a true swing.

The next step is to become thoroughly familiar with the feel of a good swinging motion. To do this, take some more practice swings and observe yourself as you perform the swing. Get thoroughly familiar with how it feels, what makes it tick, its characteristics. It's one thing for us to say it, *but you have to learn it for yourself.* We're going to assume, for the moment, that you're swinging correctly. (We'll take care of problems a bit later.)

Here are some of the things you should feel as you swing the club back and through. Don't try to feel these all at once; try for one "feel" per practice swing.

Backswing Feels:

1. Feel the forearms swing the hands away. This is the primary feel of the swing. The hands should feel as though they have been loaded with weight—and they are, in a sense, because you have loaded them with the weight of the club. You should feel the club weight with your "feelers," the forefingers and thumbs.
2. Feel how the swinging action keeps the left arm extended as it was at address.
3. Feel the arms and hands swing the club back as one unit.
4. Feel the shoulders turn in response to and in unison with the swing of the arms and club.
5. Feel the buildup of a slight tension on the inside of the right thigh; this is what triggers the recoil action.

6. Feel the weight shift from an even distribution between the feet in the set to where the weight is more forward and on the inside of the left foot and the inside and rear of the right foot just before the change of direction of the swing.
7. Feel the buildup of a slight tension in the muscles in the left side of the back just before the club changes directions. This starts the downward swing of the arms.
8. Feel the weight of the swinging club cock or bend the wrists slightly just before the club changes directions. This cocking action enables you to blend the backswing and downswing into one continuous motion.

Downswing Feels:
1. Feel the forearms swing the hands and club down and through, and feel how the wrists uncock by themselves.
2. Feel the recoil and drive of the legs.
3. Feel the extended left arm.
4. Feel the shoulders uncoiling in response to the arm swing.
5. Feel the weight shift to the heel and outside of the left foot and the ball and inside of the right foot in the finish.

Now, as you gain more experience with the swinging action, you should try to feel one portion of the body throughout the swing. Feel the forearms swinging the hands and club, feel the shoulder turn, feel the leg action, feel the foot action, but feel them *back and through*. You'll start building "whole swing" feels that will stand you in good stead the rest of your golfing life. *The ultimate goal is to realize that if you set up properly, and start the club back with a swinging action by the forearms of the hands and club, the rest of the swing will pretty much look after itself.* But this realization won't come immediately; it takes work on your part, and you'll make some mistakes along the way.

Now let's consider some characteristics of the true swinging action. These are not so much to be felt as observed at this point, but they do lead to "feels," too.

1. When the club swings back and through, *both ends of the club should swing in the same direction* at any one point in time. Now, obviously, the clubhead will swing a greater distance than the handle because it is traveling in a larger arc; nevertheless, both arcs should move in the same direction. If the clubhead and handle end ever travel in different directions, then you are applying leverage.

2. When you swing the club back, the clubhead will swing back inside the target line, then on the downswing it will approach the ball

If the clubhead and handle end of the club ever travel in different directions, as shown here, then you are applying leverage. In the true swing, both ends of the club swing in the same direction. Compare the illustration here with that on page 46.

from the inside, be square at the ball position, and then swing back to the inside of the target line again. This basic pattern is true of all straight shots. The "inside-to-square-to-inside" pattern, as we call it, is caused by the shoulders turning back and then through in response to the swing. If you can't see the pattern, put down a club parallel to the target line but a little farther away from you than where you are swinging the club through. It will soon be apparent to you.

3. In a true swing, *the length of the backward swing is the same as that of the forward swing.* The golf swing—it's especially easy to appreciate this in the "mini-swing"—is like the measured to and fro swing of the pendulum on a grandfather clock. If the backward and forward swings are of unequal length, then you're not swinging!

4. *A good swinging action times itself.* Once you have initiated a true swinging motion, it almost acquires a life of its own, one that demands you continue it to its logical conclusion. Again, it's like the tick-tock of the grandfather clock.

5. *The golf swing has a rhythm of its own.* As you swing the club away, the club swings slowly as the swing gradually overcomes inertia. Then it picks up a little speed until the change of direction. As the wrists cock, the club slows down again, waiting for the recoil action. As the downward swing of the arms starts, the clubhead is moving slowly; then, as the recoil action starts to take effect, it accelerates the clubhead

so that you achieve maximum clubhead speed at impact. The clubhead again slows down in the follow-through. The backswing is slow to fast to slow and the downswing also goes from slow to fast to slow. *This slow-to-fast-to-slow, slow-to-fast-to-slow rhythm is the heartbeat of the swing.*

These five characteristics of the swing can also be invaluable "early warning systems" that alert you when you deviate from a pure swinging action.

Ironing Out the Rough Spots

If you've been swinging your 7-iron along with us—if you haven't, you've been wasting your time and ours—as we described the feel and characteristics of a true swing, you have undoubtedly been correcting your action and refining it as we went along. Nevertheless, even those of you who have acquired a good idea of what the swing is all about may be conscious of some little tight spots developing in your action. Some of you may even be saying, I don't know what you guys are talking about! If you fall into the latter class, don't despair! Rome wasn't built in a day, and neither is a golf swing.

Now let's study the problems that can prevent a swinging action or arrest it.

Too Tight a Hold. Undoubtedly the most common reason for lack of swing, among men especially, is a tight hold. While some golfers give it the "death grip" with both hands, the worst offender is usually the right hand among naturally right-handed golfers. When you freeze the right hand, you also freeze the right wrist and elbow. A locked right elbow means that the right arm is carried back in much the same position as at address and through in the same position. This gives you a "push-back, push-through" action that is not a swing. All you have to work with are the big muscles of the upper arms and shoulders, and you will remember we told you earlier that these muscles must respond to the swinging action—they can't initiate one.

We would add that those who tend to "tight-grip" with the right hand are often those who inadvertently stand up to the ball with the left arm slack and the right arm rigid. Again, this results in a "push" action.

There's another way you can fall into the "push" action, and that is by trying to steer the club or trying to swing the club along any particular line. We've told you the shape of the arc on a correct swing (inside-to-square-to-inside), but that does not mean you should try to make it describe that path. You have to *let* the arc result from the swinging of the club and the shoulder turn that occurs as a result of the swing.

One sure indication that you're "pushing" instead of swinging is the absence of wrist action. If there is no wrist action, then you know that you are holding the club too tightly.

Things to check: You're *holding* the club gently, not gripping it tightly. The position of both arms at the address is correct—left arm firm, right arm relaxed.

Too Sloppy a Hold. This normally comes in just two varieties, thank goodness! Either the left hand is not holding the club firmly enough or both hands have too slack a hold.

LEFT HAND SLACK When the left hand is not holding firmly enough, the tendency is to pick up the club with the right hand. This will cause the clubhead to be traveling to the right while the butt end of the club goes to the left. Yes, this is leverage, and it violates one of the basic characteristics of the swing, that both ends of the club should travel in the same direction. You can test for this quite easily by going a little way back in the backswing and stopping. If the clubhead is well to the right of the hands and the butt end is pointing to the left leg or beyond it, then you are picking the club up instead of swinging. Because of the "pick-up" action in the hands, there will be no shoulder turn—so the lack of shoulder turn can be an indicator of this problem, too.

Things to check: Firm up the hold in the left hand, check your "left shoulder set," and be very conscious during the swing that both ends of the club are traveling in the same direction. See that you're not trying consciously to cock the wrists; any wrist cock must be the *result* of the swinging action.

BOTH HANDS SLACK When both hands hold the club too loosely, you get a "flip-flop" action in the wrists. The club is "dragged" away and, in its most extreme form, the sole of the club will actually drag along the ground. What usually happens then is a quick pickup of the club with the wrists, again no shoulder turn to speak of, and in the downswing probably a "scooping up" action with the wrists.

Things to check: Obviously, you have to firm up the hold in both hands. You have to hold the club firmly enough to control it, but not to the point where you are "tight-gripping" it. There is a happy medium.

We would add one more thing to the too tight-too sloppy hold problems. It's been our experience that while many men tend to "tight-grip" the club, very few women err in this way. Women, if anything, tend to be the golfers with too sloppy a hold—although some men fall into the habit, usually as a result of trying to correct a "tight-grip" situation.

Although it is rare to have too slack a hold with the right hand, it is possible. If the left hand is holding firmly enough, you can make a pretty good arc to the swing even if the right hand is slack because, as we've said, the left arm makes the arc. However, when the right hand does not hold firmly enough, you are in effect taking the right arm out of the swing, and you'll lose power. You should check your "towel-twisting" pressure periodically to make certain that both hands are doing their job.

No Recoil. If you swing back and find that you have to make a conscious effort to swing through, then there's been no recoil. If there's no recoil, there's obviously been no coil, and the reason for that is that your legs are slack and purposeless.

Things to check: Reread the passage on "leg set" and make certain your right knee is set inward a little more than the left. The *feeling* you should have is one of gripping the ground with the insides of your feet and legs. You should feel as if nothing could push you over. The set in the legs and the body generally should be similar to the one you would adopt if you were holding a heavy weight in front of you.

Now that we've made any necessary corrections, and tested them with a few practice swings, let's get to hitting some balls with the mini-swing.

The Mini-swing in Action

As you have been making these practice swings with the mini-swing and acquiring some proficiency with the swinging action, you will have noticed, on the downswing, the club clipping the grass starting at a point a little to the right of your left heel. That point at which the club has been entering the grass is just before the low point in your swing arc. Set the ball down in relation to the feet with the center of the ball right on the line where the "clipping" action started. In this way you will be contacting the ball a little before the low point in the swing arc, ensuring a more solid hit on the ball.

Assuming you're set at the ball now, make a couple of waggles to free up a little, and while you're doing so, run through your mind the feel of the swinging action. Once you have that clear in your mind, set the club behind the ball and swing.

We have no way of knowing how your first few swings will be. If you're lucky, and there's a sweet little click as the ball is swept away in the path of the swing, and you find yourself in the correct follow-through position you've been practicing, then stop right there and hold that position. Your mind will have registered the feel of that good swing, as though it had taken a movie of it. So "rewind the reel" and play it again in your mind. Remember, this is how a good golf swing feels to you—and that feel is precious.

We say this because all too often a golfer at practice will become excited when he makes a good swing that results in a well-hit ball. He will immediately put down another ball and hit it quickly. The second shot, because it was rushed and made without adequate mental preparation, will probably be a disappointment. Another ball is put down quickly, another swing, another miss, and soon that good swing is almost irretrievable.

Remember: As a general rule, never hit a lot of balls rapidly in succession. Play each shot and make each swing as though it were for the Open. And when you make a good swing, stop! Project the mental movie of that good swing again and again in your mind, and you'll find yourself using that mental image to make your next swing a good one.

If you're having some difficulty in swinging smoothly, remember that we did warn you that the ball can induce a condition of being "ball-bound," in which you tend to hit at the ball instead of swinging through it. In other words, your practice swing was fine, but you can't hit a ball with it! What has happened is that not only your eyes but your whole mind has locked onto the ball, leaving no part of the mind to attend to the business of swinging the club.

The remedy is simple. You're going to have to de-emphasize looking at the ball for the moment and concentrate more attention on the swing. Set up properly and make a couple of practice swings with the brushing action while returning to the primary feel of the swing—swinging the hands and club with the forearms. Retaining that feel, set up to the ball, and then deliberately squint your eyes a little so that the ball is now slightly blurred. Make the swing—and chances are that this swing will be a good one, at least much better that what you've done before. Repeat a few times before trying a swing with eyes focused on the ball.

Don't get us wrong; in a good swing, you do look at the ball. Later, concentration on the ball can even free you to make a good swing. But when you're learning the swing, you have to pay attention to the swinging motion. It's more important that you are making a good swing, and then merely observing how this good swing incidentally sweeps the ball off somewhere in its path. If you're still having difficulty making a good swing when the ball is there, then you need further sensitizing to the feel of a true swinging action between swings at the ball. Here are two methods to accomplish that.

Using the "Swing Weight." Take out your weight on a string (the "Swing Weight") and your 7-iron. Holding the club in your left hand, just below the grip, lay the end of the string along the grip of the club. Lightly hold the end of the grip with the forefinger and thumb of the right hand; the thumb will be holding the end of the string against the

An excellent way to acquire the feel of a swinging action is to swing the "Swing Weight" and 7-iron together. Hold the end of the grip between the forefinger and thumb, pinching the end of the string against the grip. Now swing the two back and forth together (A and B). While it is possible to move the club through an arc by means of leverage (C), it is plainly a less efficient motion. Notice that, with a leverage action, the "Swing Weight" doesn't move.

grip. Now stand up and let the club and the "Swing Weight" hang down vertically.

What we want you to do is to start swinging the club and the "Swing Weight" back and forth *together*. This is not as easy as it may seem. At first you may well be jerking the club, or trying to push or pull it back, but you will soon convince yourself of the futility of this, for the "Swing Weight" will not swing with the club unless you make a true swinging motion. Once you get them swinging together, keep on swinging back and forth and run through your mind the characteristics of the swing that apply here: Both ends of the club are swinging together, the backward and forward halves of the arc are of equal length, the feel of the centrifugal force occurs in the finger and thumb, and so on.

Now we want you to induce "wrong" motions in the combo. And the reason for this is very simple: Unless you can learn to distinguish between a true swing and the various wrong motions, which we call leverage, you will never advance as a golfer. You must experience both right and wrong.

The first type of wrong motion is where you literally use your forefingers and thumbs as levers. By exerting pressure first with the forefinger and then the thumb you can move the club through an arc, but this is a far less efficient motion than the true swing, as you will plainly see, and, since the "Swing Weight" hangs straight down all the time you're levering, it's obvious that there is no sort of swinging motion. Notice also that each end of the club is traveling in a different direction.

The second type of wrong motion is a "push-pull" action. Again, it's not a swing. Instead of the "Swing Weight" and the club swinging together, they may well go in opposite directions. Notice the new pressures that appear in the forefingers and thumbs as you push and pull. And notice that there's a tendency for leverage to develop. The two types of wrong motion are related.

Here we would like to add a point that many of our pupils have found useful: If you lose the swing, nine times out of ten you "lose" it right at the start of the backswing. If you search your own memories as a golfer, you'll remember having had the experience where you started the swing, and even though you had swung the club only a few feet back, you *knew* that the shot would be a good one. Conversely, how many times have you hit a bad shot and moaned, I *knew* I was going to miss that one! In one case, of course, you started with a true swinging motion, and in the other you introduced some sort of leverage. However, the major reason why so many of our pupils lose the swing, we have found, is anxiety. They want to get the club swinging at all costs, so they jerk or pressure the club.

The secret of starting the swing correctly is to make certain you start smoothly and rhythmically, applying the force *gradually*. You may remember when swinging the "Swing Weight" in a circle about your hand (described in the first chapter of this book) how *gradually* you had to apply the force with your forearm in order to get the "Swing Weight" swinging. But eventually you did get it swinging; you just had to have a little patience and not succumb to jerky, leverage-type pressures to get it going. It's exactly the same with the golf swing. You must start the swing smoothly, gradually, and with patience to overcome the inertia of the club. Whatever your natural tempo, the start of the swing must feel "slow" to you—remember the "slow-to-fast" rhythm we told you about earlier? As Bobby Jones once said, "No golfer ever swung back too slowly!"

Now we'd like you to repeat these experiments using the left hand, so that both hands get a better idea of their roles in the swing.

Non-stop Swinging. The second way to sensitize yourself to a true swing is by means of what we call "non-stop swinging." This is simply swinging back and forth in one continuous motion, a favorite exercise of golfers for years. However, the only problem with what average golfers do is that they only swing back and forth a couple of times. We're talking about swinging at least 10 and as many as 20 times back and forth without a pause. (Keep the length of the swing to about that of the mini-swing, and don't worry if you make a slightly larger swing every so often—in effect you'll be sneaking up on the half-swing, our next goal!)

When you're learning the swing, you'll find that you need as many as a half-dozen back and forth motions before you sense that you are truly swinging the club. Consider what would have happened if you had stopped at one or two: *You never would have felt the true swing!*

Once you have the club swinging freely, we want you to zero in again on the feels and characteristics of a true swinging action. The primary feel we want you to concentrate on is that of the forearms swinging the club back and forth. But what we'd like you to do is to start with this primary feel and then switch your attention for a couple of swings or so to such feels as the shoulders turning in response to the swing, the legs working with the swing, the wrists cocking and uncocking freely, and so on. Then switch back to the primary feel—and keep on swinging. After a few minutes of non-stop swinging you'll be pleasantly surprised at how, almost in spite of yourself, the quality of the

swing has improved. Whether it's your freedom of swing, your rhythm.
your tempo—whatever characteristic of the true swing you think of—all
will have made quantum leaps forward. And, we may add, in a relatively
"painless" fashion!

Now what we would like you to do is to alternate these two methods of sensitizing yourself to the swing with hitting balls with the mini-
swing. And to help bridge any gap in feel, we suggest that you take a
couple of "brushing" practice swings before each stroke at the ball.

By now you should be performing the mini-swing pretty well. Of
course, every now and then a wrong motion will creep in and you'll lose
the swing. Don't be too hard on yourself when this occurs. *Just concentrate on making the next swing a good one.* As long as you play golf, you
are going to make wrong motions from time to time—and the golf shot
that results will be spoiled to some extent. That is why even the experts
like Jack Nicklaus or Johnny Miller will occasionally miss shots, they
simply "put a bad swing on the ball," as the saying is. What the experts
do achieve however, is to make fewer bad swings than do average
golfers, because they know the feel of a true swinging action, have
experienced it many times, and can reproduce it practically every time.
And that is what you should aim for, too.

To conclude this section on the mini-swing, we would like to make
one further suggestion. Now that you know the difference between a
free swinging motion and the "leverage" type motions, don't spend any
more time on feeling the wrong motions. Knowing right from wrong is
important when you're learning the swing, and it will help you to find
out what has gone wrong when you're off your game. But for now,
simply practice what is right. Set up to the ball correctly and swing the
hands and club with the forearms. You will find that the true, free
swinging action will flow from these two basics.

Advancing to the Half-swing

The half-swing is simply an extension of the mini-swing. In the
mini-swing you swung back until the hands just cleared the right leg on
the backswing, and then through to a point where the hands just cleared
the left leg. In the half-swing. you swing back until the hands are about
hip high and then through until the hands are again hip high.

There are no essential differences between the mini-swing and the
half-swing. And this is one of the biggest benefits to the golfer of learning the swing by our method: *In learning the mini-swing you have, in
effect, learned the golf swing.* As you progress to the full swing, the feel

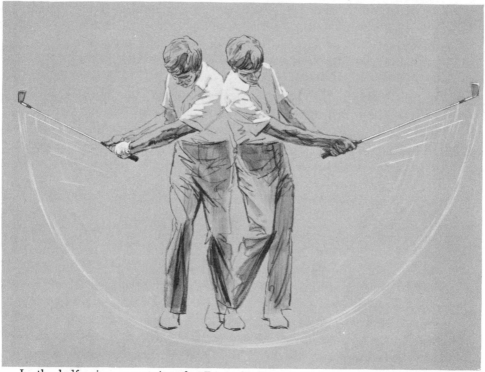

In the half-swing, you swing the 7-iron back until the hands are about hip high, and swing through until again the hands are about hip high.

will be the same, the characteristics will be the same—they're just amplified somewhat.

Before we make the half-swing, a few changes will be necessary to accommodate the longer swing. First, instead of holding the club at the extreme lower end of the grip, move up the grip half an inch, so that a little of the grip appears below the right hand. Second, you will need a slightly wider stance. To achieve this, simply move the right foot from the "feet together" position a little farther to the right than before; a couple of inches should do the trick. The wider stance enables you to keep your balance during the longer swing, which will generate more centrifugal force than the mini-swing. It also permits the legs to respond more vigorously to the bigger swinging action, as they should. The only other adjustment is to stand a little taller to the ball. Because you have made the club, in effect, a little longer, you won't have to bend forward as much as before.

In the same way that we approached the mini-swing with a few "dry runs," or practice swings, we think it important to start our study of the half-swing, similarly and for the same reason. The ball can be a distraction and can occupy too much of the mind while you're learning the movement. Take a few practice swings now and let's check what's happening.

As you swing the hands and club back with the forearms to the halfway point, feel the weight of the swinging club in your "feelers." The swinging action will again keep the left arm extended, and there will be the feel of the arms and hands swinging the club away as a unit. However, due to the longer swing, the shoulders, hips, and legs will make a bigger response.

In the mini-swing, the shoulders made only a small turn. In the half-swing, they have to make a bigger turn, of around 45 degrees. The hips, which hardly had to move in the mini-swing, will make a larger turn this time, and there will be a larger movement in the legs. The left knee will be pulled forward and to the right a little, and the right thigh will be pulled backward a little by the turn of the right hip. There will also be a larger weight shift: The weight will move more to the ball and inside the front portion of the left foot than before and there will be more weight on the inside and back of the right foot. At the change in direction of the swing, there will be a slight additional bend in the right arm compared to its position in the set, and because of the slightly increased speed of swing, a slightly increased wrist cock. The toe of the club should point skyward.

Coil/recoil is also magnified in the half-swing. There's more stretching of the muscles in the left side of the back by the bigger shoulder turn, and there's more tension created on the inside muscles of the right leg. The result, of course, is that there will be a faster arm swing down and through the ball area and increased thrust by the legs in the downswing. Thus you should finish with most of your weight on the outside and back of the left foot, the right heel will be up, and only the inside of the ball of the foot will be on the ground. The right knee will kick in more than before, and the hips and shoulders will have turned more than in the mini-swing. The arms and the club will be extended toward the hole, and again the toe of the club should point skyward.

As you practice the half-swing, continue to check that the feels and characteristics we described in the mini-swing are present in your half-swing. If problems develop, consult the sections on the hold and lack of coil/recoil. Now we would like to make some additional points that will be helpful.

Points to Watch

As the swing gets larger, most golfers we've taught tend to try to "overcontrol" the action. It's almost as though they're afraid of the force they're developing and fear that it will get out of control and run away from them. This can lead to two problems: First, the golfer will tend to lift the clubhead with his hands and arms rather than swing back. Second, if he does coil and otherwise swing back correctly, he's afraid to "let everything go" or release in the follow-through.

There are several ways to attack the first problem and at the same time help you achieve a free swinging action. The first is our old friend, the "brushing" action: Take several practice half-swings, brushing back for six inches and through for six inches. This will quickly reestablish the correct swinging action. Remember: The brushing action is always something you can fall back on when you lose the swing. That's why we position it at the beginning of our method. The second way is the "non-stop" swing: As you swing back and forth, check that you're swinging freely and that the shoulders and legs are responding correctly in both directions. The third way is really an extension of the second. When we're on the lesson tee we have on hand an old club—a short iron of any sort will do—which we've weighted with lead tape so that it's two or three times the weight of a normal club. We ask pupils to swing this club with the "non-stop" swing, and very soon they realize the futility of trying to lift or push the club back and through. They must let the shoulders and legs respond to the swing—otherwise, they can hardly move it! Anyone can make himself such a practice club, and we urge you to do it.

To help you when you're swinging a regular club, we suggest you think of "swinging the triangle." When you set up to the ball, your arms and a line across your shoulders form a triangle shape. Now, when you swing the club back with your forearms, think of maintaining that triangle shape. This will almost force the shoulders to respond to and turn with the arm swing, both back and through.

There's just one caution we have to add to the "triangle" image. A few of our pupils will overdo the "triangle" to the point where they lock the right arm going back and the left arm in the finish. This is not the idea! If you lock the right arm going back, you'll be in effect "pushing" the club back. And if you lock the left elbow in the finish, you'll inhibit the free release of the forearms. The triangle image is useful as a way of ensuring that the shoulders turn in response to the swing, but you must allow the arms to function naturally!

In the case of the second problem, holding back in the follow-through, the "non-stop" swing, the heavy club, and the "triangle" image can all help. However, there are two aspects of the release that can still "stick." One is a free swing-through of the hands, wrists, and forearms. Your first indication of this problem would be stiffened wrists and a sharp tug on the fingers of the left hand in the follow-through. If this happens to you, check the position of the clubface in the finish. The toe of the club should be pointing directly to the sky (straight up).

The second sticking point is the right leg. If you find it difficult to swing the club through to hip high, or the club "sticks" or stops at a lower level than the hips in the finish, that's a sure sign you have not released the right leg. Check where your right knee has finished. It should point in front of the ball's original position.

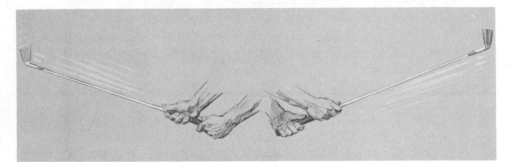

A good way to condition yourself to the correct release is to swing with the hands separated an inch or so apart on the grip. This exercise helps you develop both the correct release of the forearms, wrists and hands and the release of the right leg and side.

A good way to condition yourself to the correct release of the forearms, wrists, and hands is to take the regular hold on the club with the left hand at the top of the grip and hold the bottom of the grip with all the fingers of the right hand. Your hands will then be separated on the grip by about an inch. Now, when you swing back and through, you should have no difficulty in finishing in the correct toe-up position. The "hands separated" exercise will make holding back the club a practical impossibility; your hands will "fly" through the hitting area into the finish. (If you still have difficulty, separate your hands a little farther apart.)

The "hands separated" drill can also help with freeing the release of the right leg and side. Swing the club back and through, making a determination to coordinate the right knee with the arm swing through the impact area and on into the follow-through. If necessary, use the heavy club "hands separated" style to get the desired effect.

Here we would like to make the point that any fear of a free release is unwarranted. When you make a free swing and a free release you are generating plenty of centrifugal force. *That is precisely what you want!* The centrifugal force is what keeps the swing true and the clubface in the correct position for a powerful hit on the ball. *When you fight centrifugal force by stiffening up, you lose the swing, you lose the force, and you lose—not gain—accuracy.* It's like a spinning top: The faster it spins, the steadier it is.

The truth of what we're saying will be immediately apparent to you when you hit balls with the half-swing. A free swing and a free release will "drill" the ball straight down the middle. Anything less than a free swing—and certainly if you try to hold back, steer, or otherwise try to control the finish—the result will be less distance and less accurate shots. Remember: The ball can only react to the action you make. Make yours a swinging action, with nothing held back.

In practicing the half-swing with a ball, adopt the same general procedure as with the mini-swing. Intersperse hitting the ball with plenty of "non-stop" swinging and the other sensitizing exercise with the "Swing Weight." You can even take the exercise with the "Swing Weight" a stage closer to the actual swing. Here's how:

Lay the end of the string down the grip of your 7-iron and adopt the regular hold over both the string and the grip and set up for the half-swing. Now swing back and forth "non-stop" fashion. Not easy to do, perhaps, but it can only improve the quality of your swing—and that's the name of our game!

The Three-quarter Swing

In the same way that the half-swing was an extension of the mini-swing, so the three-quarter swing is simply an extension of the half-swing. In the half-swing, you swung the hands back to hip height and through to hip height; in the three-quarter swing, you swing the hands back to shoulder height and through to shoulder height.

Again, there are no essential differences between the three-quarter swing and either the half-swing or the quarter-swing. Only the length of the swing is longer. All the basics of the set and the free swing still apply.

In the three-quarter swing, you swing the 7-iron back until the hands are at shoulder height, and swing through until again the hands are at shoulder height.

Before we make the three-quarter swing, a few changes are necessary at the setup position. Move the hold up the grip another half inch or so from where you held it for the half-swing; once again you're making the club in effect a little longer, and this of itself will increase the width of the arc. To allow for the club's being a little longer, stand a little taller to the ball. To accommodate the longer swing, the increased centrifugal force, and the increased leg and foot action, you should again widen the stance a little from the "feet together" position by moving the right foot two inches or so to the right.

Before we go any further, we would like to make one point that applies generally to width of stance: Don't take our recommendations on how far apart to spread the feet as being "set in stone." They're not the Ten Commandments; they're simply a rough guide and a way of getting across the principle that, as the swing becomes longer, your stance should be widened slightly to accommodate it. If you feel more comfortable with a *slightly* wider or narrower stance—this will become apparent to you as you work with each of the lengths of swing we're describing here—then feel free to adopt it. However, don't overdo any such personal variations. Too wide a stance will tend to lock the legs and prevent their natural response to the swing. Too narrow a stance will mean loss of balance.

Now let's take a few practice three-quarter swings and check the action.

Swing the hands and club back with the forearms with the thought that this time you're going to swing up to shoulder height. Again the swinging action will keep the left arm extended and there will be the feel of the arms and hands swinging the club away as a unit. Due to the longer swing, the shoulders will turn almost fully away from the target. The hips will also make a larger turn, and there will be a bigger response in the legs. The left knee will be pulled forward and to the right farther than before and the right thigh will be pulled back farther with the movement of the right hip directly backwards. There will be more of a weight shift: In the left foot the weight will move farther forward to the inside of the ball of the foot, and there will be more weight on the inside and rear of the right foot.

As you reach the top of the swing, the arms will swing back higher than before, to the height of the shoulders and in line with the right shoulder—or slightly closer to the neck, depending on your physique. The left arm will remain extended and the right arm will bend more into a recognizable "ready for the throw" position. Due to the increased momentum resulting from the longer swing, there will be increased cocking action in the wrists. The club will swing up to where it points straight up in the air (as seen from in front of the player) and a little beyond.

There will be more coil/recoil, too; more stretching of the muscles in the left side of the back because of the increased shoulder turn; more tension created in the inside muscles of the right leg; a faster arm swing through the ball; and more leg thrust. The increased momentum of the swing will carry you through the half-swing finish position and on upward until you finish in a position where practically all the weight is on the outside of the heel of the left foot, the right knee points in front of the original ball position, the right heel has lifted, and the whole right foot has turned so that there's just a little weight left on the inside of the right big toe area. You will be standing pretty much erect, your left arm will have folded, and there may be a little folding in the right arm, too. Your hands will be in line with the left shoulder (or slightly closer to the neck if yours is a more upright swing) and the club will be in more or less a "mirror" position to that at the top.

Now do a stint of "non-stop" swinging. Get the feel of this three-quarter swing into your system—and emphasize a free arm swing back and through. Remember: We have, for clarity, given you a lot of detail about the correct swing, such as wrist cock, shoulder turn, hip turn, and leg action, but it's important to keep reminding yourself that *the free swing creates the "details,"* not the other way around. *Don't fall into the trap of trying to make happen what you should let happen.* You can tick off one by one the points we have given you about the three-quarter swing as you swing back and forth, *but don't stop swinging!*

The Feel of the "Swing Center"

While executing the "non-stop" swing, you should continue to check the feels and characteristics of a true swing that we've given you. And now you are ready for another feel of the free swing that we consider very important: The "Swing Center."

You may remember, when you were whirling the "Swing Weight" around your hand, our talking about the center or zero point of the swing. We pointed out that the forefinger and thumb were not the center of the swinging action, that it was somewhere in the upper arm region. In the same way, the hands are not the center of the golf swing. They (and the club) are what you swing with the forearms, but the centrifugal force you generate will find a center or zero point, via the hands, arms, and shoulders, in the body. It is this center of the swing, or "Swing Center," that we now want you to feel.

We choose to introduce you to the "Swing Center" at this point because the three-quarter swing with a 7-iron is one of the best means of feeling it. And the method is simply the "non-stop" swing.

Get set for the three-quarter swing and begin swinging the club back and through. Once the club is truly swinging, feel the centrifugal force and try to be aware that you are swinging this force from a center. After a while, you should feel the "Swing Center" in your spine at a point somewhere in the small of the back. As you continue swinging, you will be aware that this "Swing Center" doesn't move.

If you have difficulty feeling your "Swing Center," it's an indication that you have broken your chain of connection somewhere between the hands and the "Swing Center." Check your left arm set, which connects the left arm to the shoulders, and make certain the legs and shoulders are responding to the swing. If the shoulders are not turning with the swing, then you're probably picking up the club instead of swinging it back. If you pick up the club and allow the left arm to bend, this will break your connections and you'll have no feeling of the "Swing Center." Use the "triangle" image to keep the shoulders and arms working together.

Another area where your connections can break down is in the hands. If the hands open toward the end of the backswing—if the palm of the right hand comes away from the left thumb—this can also prevent your feeling the "Swing Center." Check to see that you've applied the light "towel-twisting" pressure of one hand toward the other.

As you find us repeating a number of points about the true swing, you'll appreciate that feeling your "Swing Center" is one of the best *tests* that the swing you are making is free and correct. However, your consciousness of the "Swing Center" does two things for you in particular: If you're truly aware of your "Swing Center," it becomes impossible for you to "sway," that is, to make lateral movements to the right on the backswing. Why? Because once you're aware of the "Swing Center," any swaying action will sound an alarm bell in your head as you feel your "Swing Center" dissolve, so to speak, from a solid feel to "no-feel" as you move to the right. It also becomes impossible for you to "over-swing" going back; by this we mean such false actions as bending the left arm, consciously working the legs and hips in a spinning action which destroys the coiling action, or even relaxing the hold at the top of the swing. The only way you can feel your "Swing Center" is by establishing your connections in the set and then swinging freely, maintaining your connections.

Some of you may still be finding it difficult to feel your "Swing Center." We know it's not easy, so here's a little additional help: Set up for the three-quarter swing, waggle a couple of times, and then close your eyes. Now do a stint of "non-stop" swinging with the eyes still closed. (Even though you're not hitting a ball at the moment, much of your brain can be occupied with simply seeing. By swinging with your eyes closed, you will heighten your perception and awareness of your body as it is swinging.) Most of you will now be able to feel your "Swing Center." If you still cannot, then, as a temporary expedient, press your weighted club into service. Close your eyes and swing the weighted club with the "non-stop" swing, and all of you will soon feel your "Swing Center."

As you move now to hitting balls with the three-quarter swing, adopt the same procedure as before. Hit a few balls, then take time out for a spell of "non-stop" swinging. Hit some more balls, take some more time out for a swing-sensitizing stint. And so on.

If you're dissatisfied with the way you're striking the ball, yet you feel the quality of your swing is really good, it could be an indication that you should pay more attention to the ball and the target. Set up to the ball, having made a clear picture in your mind of the ball's traveling to the target and of the swing that will get the job done. Now just come back to the ball with your eyes and concentrate your gaze on the exact spot on the back of the ball that you want to hit. Swing back, making a determination in your mind that you will see the club strike the ball exactly as planned. If the shot is unsatisfactory, it indicates that your swing needs more work. If the shot goes off straight as an arrow, *it shows that the true swing is starting to become a conditioned response.* So now, when you hit balls, just think of the target and the ball. And only think of the swing exclusively when working on the swing—performing "non-stop" swings or swing exercises.

The Full Swing

Now we come to the full swing. Again, you should think of it as simply a longer version of the quarter-, half-, and three-quarter swings. All the basics of the set and the free swing we've previously discussed still apply. Nothing has changed except that in the full swing, you swing the hands over the right shoulder going back, and to a point over the left shoulder in the follow-through (or slightly closer to the neck in both cases if your natural swing plane is more upright).

Again, in line with our previous practice, there are a few changes at address. Move the hold up to the top of the grip so that the side of the butt of the left hand is level to the cap end of the grip. What we don't want is to have any part of the butt of the left hand off the grip—this can lead to looseness in the swing. All of the butt of the left hand must be on the grip so that the "forefinger to the butt" balance can be made comfortably. (If you do feel compelled to hold the club with part of the butt of the hand off the grip, it could be an indication that you need slightly longer clubs.) And, again, stand a little taller to the ball and widen the stance another few inches.

As before, let's take a few practice swings with the full swing and check what's happening. Swing the hands and club away with the forearms while thinking that you are going to swing the hands up over the right shoulder. As you swing back, note that the left arm stays extended naturally just from the momentum of the swing and the shoulders turning "triangle" fashion with the swing of the arms. In swinging your

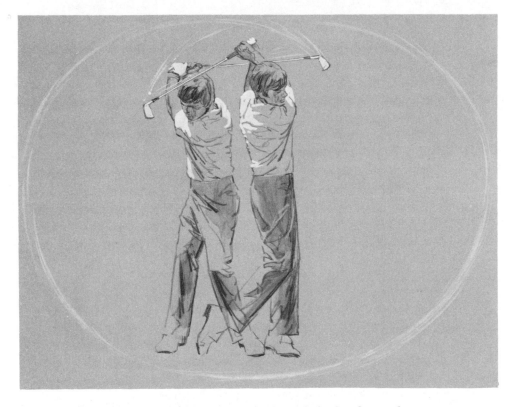

In the full swing, you swing the 7-iron back until the hands are about over the right shoulder, and swing through until the hands are about over the left shoulder.

hands to the top, the shoulders will have to make a larger turn than before. In the full swing, you should make as full a shoulder turn as possible. You should "turn your back" on the hole; the shoulders will turn 90 degrees or more if you are supple. Because of the bigger shoulder turn, the legs will respond more. The left knee will be pulled forward and to the right behind the ball, and the right thigh will be pulled back farther than before, resulting in a hip turn of around 45 degrees. There will be more weight shift. Your weight will travel farther forward to the inside of the ball of the left foot and you may find that your left heel comes just a little off the ground. There will be more weight on the inside and rear of the right foot.

Let's enlarge a little on the foot action: Whether your left heel will lift or not is purely a function of how supple you are. Many people can make a full swing with the 7-iron without the left heel's rising at all. If that's the case, fine. If the left heel has to rise a little, that's fine too. Let the left foot work as a result of the swing; don't fall into the error of deliberately lifting the left heel—that will cause the hips to turn too far and destroy the coiling action. Nor should you fight a natural rise of the left heel; this tightens the spring of the coil so tightly that you would tend to spin the hips in the downswing, throwing the clubhead outside the correct swing line.

As you reach the top of the swing, your arms will swing back higher than before—to a point over the "right-shoulder-to-middle-of-neck" area. The right arm will fold more than before. There will also be maximum cocking of the wrists due to the increased momentum of the club. The club will swing up until it is about parallel to the ground, and it will lie on a line parallel to the target line.

Here again, the precise point to which you swing back is personal. Different degrees of suppleness in the waist, shoulders, wrists, and hands may mean your own individual full backswing length may fall short of or go slightly past what we have described. No matter; if yours is a true swinging action, you will soon establish your ideal backswing length.

Since you have achieved maximum coil, the recoil will be at its maximum, too. There will be a faster arm swing down and a greater leg drive through the ball. In the finish, your hands will swing up over your left shoulder (or a corresponding point closer to the neck if your swing is more upright) and the club will finish behind your back; you will be erect with the hips and chest area facing to the left of the target; and imaginary lines across the shoulders and hips would be at about right angles to the target line. All your weight will be on the outside of the heel of the left foot and only the toe of the right shoe will be on the ground. Again, your right leg should release so that the right knee points in front of the original ball position.

Now we would like you to do some "non-stop" swinging to become familiar with the full swing. Observe the points we've been describing, but remember to keep *swinging freely*. Convince yourself that it is the free swing that creates weight shift, shoulder turn, leg action, and wrist cock. Then hit some balls with the same swinging action.

Testing Your Swinging Action

At this point it is important for you to check the quality of your swinging action in the full swing. You may remember our pointing out in the mini-swing that if the butt end of the club travels in a different direction than the clubhead end then you are leveraging the club, not swinging it. This was easy to see in the mini-swing because you were holding the club at the bottom end of the grip and a good portion of the grip projected up above your hands.

You can get the same effect in the full swing by choking down on the longest club in your bag, the driver. Hold your driver at the bottom end of the grip and make a few practice swings—full swings—to get the feel of it. To test your action, swing back as though you were going to make a full swing, but stop the swing at the mini-swing or quarter point in the backswing. Then apply the same tests you did in the mini-swing to see if you're truly swinging—if both ends of the club are moving together—or whether some form of leverage, such as pushing the club back or picking it up quickly, has crept into your action.

You can also test the quality of your swing through the hitting area by the same method, especially if you swing through slowly. If the butt end of the club backs away from the hole and the clubhead goes forward of the hands, that means you are trying to push the clubhead through. Remember: You can't push the clubhead through as fast as you can swing it! On the other hand, if your hands reach the position where the ball would be and the butt end of the club is way in advance of the hands and the clubhead is way behind, then it means you are blocking out the swing, that is, not allowing the hands to release. Only if both ends of the club are traveling through the ball area together are you swinging freely.

Here we want to introduce another method of testing your swinging action. In many ways it is one of the most important because it is both an active principle to work on and a warning signal that the swing has broken down. Take your 7-iron and do a stint of "non-stop" swinging. Once you're satisfied that you're swinging freely, transfer your attention to your hands and you will make this discovery: *In the true swing there are no sudden, additional pressures created in or on the hands.* Of course you start with some pressure in the last three fingers of the left hand and the middle two fingers of the right hand, but this is an even pressure, a "holding" pressure. What we have in mind are sudden additional *sideways* increases in pressure in a particular part or parts of the hands.

If, for example, you lever the club back, with the clubhead being picked up and the hands staying in the same place, you will feel additional pressure against the last three fingers and the butt of the left hand and against the forefinger of the right hand. You'll also feel additional pressures in the hands if you drag the club back or lift it back. Additional pressure will also warn you when the shoulders are not turning in response to the swing. When you do that, at a certain point you will be compelled to lift the club up—again creating additional pressure in the hands.

The same principle holds true on the downswing. If you lever the club or push the clubhead ahead of the hands, you will feel pressure in the fingertips of the left hand and you will feel the grip of the club backing up against the right palm. The basic point is that you should feel no additional *sideways* pressures in the hands during the swing. If you do, you are not swinging the club.

It is true that, as you swing the club through impact, the hold on the grip will tighten in response to the pull created on the hands by centrifugal force. However, this tightening of the hold is something you don't have to think about—it will happen by itself if you are swinging freely. The reason you can't feel it is that it is still an even, "holding" pressure; it is not an "additional" sideways pressure localized in one part or parts of the hands.

Remember the last time you hit an extraordinarily long shot— maybe a drive that never seemed to come down, or an iron shot that was drilled straight for the pin? Cast your mind back and try to remember what feeling you had in the hands. We'll bet you will say something like, I didn't feel anything happening in my hands. That may be too strong a statement—obviously you had to have hold of the club. Perhaps you really meant to say, I took my hold on the club and swung, and I noticed no additional sideways pressures during the swing. Anytime you are conscious of additional pressures, your hands have been overactive. Remember our basic principle of swinging: You swing the hands with the forearms; you don't *do* anything consciously with the hands—they just hold the club.

Forget the "Early Wrist Cock"

Here we would like to discuss an action that many teachers recently have said is desirable but which we think is confusing. It appears under various names, the most common being the "early wrist cock" or "early set of the hands." In essence, these teachers advocate cocking the wrists early in the backswing. But what they're doing is confusing an action that you should *let* happen rather than *make* happen. The wrists must be free to cock and uncock, but, as we've learned, whatever the length of your backswing, you will get the appropriate amount of cocking action in the wrists if your action is a free, true swing.

And not all the cocking action takes place at the top of the swing.

Part of it takes place on the way to the top, but if you try to actively cock the wrists, you are simply levering the club—and in so doing you cause the club to leave the arc that would be created by a pure swinging action. On the other hand, if you swing the club back, you get as wide an arc as possible, the left arm stays extended (maintaining the arc of the swing and keeping it constant), and the wrist action will be automatic.

Dick Farley recently had a conversation about this very problem with Johnny Miller, a player to whom many who teach the "early wrist cock" point as an example of what they recommend, and John Jacobs, the famous teacher from England. Johnny said that when he gets into trouble with his swing, it's when the path of his swing gets to be too much like an egg standing on end—as opposed to the ideal shape, that of an egg standing on its side. In our language, that translates into picking the club up too quickly with the hands, or leverage. Johnny also said he doesn't consciously try to pick the club up; he just tries to swing it back.

We hope that explanation will convince you of the futility of trying consciously to pick up the club in a normal backswing. We have seen many average players try it, and all they do is ruin their swings. Now, on some shots you do have to swing the club up a little quicker than usual, but that is shotmaking, an adaptation of the basic swinging action to a particular problem on the course. (We will discuss this later, under shotmaking.) For a plain, straightforward swing with any club, there should be no conscious picking up of the club.

Getting back to the "equal pressure" thought and ways of testing to determine whether you are swinging correctly or not, we should add one more point. You can rotate the hands (and with them the forearms) to the right or left (opening or closing the clubface) during the swing, and in doing you can hook or slice the ball. Doing this deliberately we will discuss later, under shotmaking, but the point here is that this rotation of the hands can occur during the swing without your being aware of it because rotating the hands doesn't create additional sideways pressure points in the hands. This could account for a lot of the curve balls you might be hitting at this point.

To learn to distinguish between the cocking of the wrists and this rotation, take your 7-iron and set up to an imaginary ball. Now stand more erect so that you lift the club a foot or so off the ground. With a pure cocking action of the wrists, the club moves straight up in the air. Do this a couple of times to get the feel of the cocking action clearly in your mind, and then return the club to the starting position. Now rotate the hands to the right, and you will see that the clubface opens. Rotate them to the left, and the clubface closes. Of course, you could compensate during the swing by making another rotation in the direction opposite to your first rotation, but this makes a complicated swing for a normal shot in which you simply want to hit the ball straight. For such a shot, there should be no rotation at all.

Testing for Hand and Arm Rotation

The best way to verify that no unwanted hand and forearm rotation has crept into your swing is to use what we call the "swing and

To check for unwanted hand and forearm rotation, use the "Swing and Stop" method. Swing back and stop at the half-swing position. If you have swung back correctly, that is, with no rotation, then the toe of the club will point directly to the sky (A). However, if the clubface points to the sky, you have rotated the clubface into an open position (B). If the clubface points to the ground, you have closed the clubface (C).

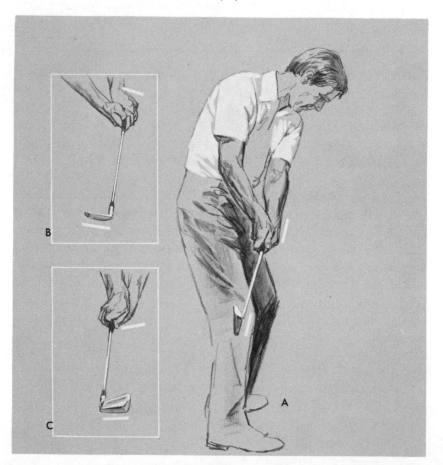

stop" method. Take your setup for the full swing with the 7-iron and swing back, but stop the club at the position you swung to for the half-swing. If you have swung back without any rotation of the hands, then the *toe* of the club will be pointing directly to the sky. However, if the *clubface* is pointing to the sky, you have rotated the clubface to the right and into an open position. If the *clubface points to the ground*, you have rotated to the left, closing the clubface. If you have fallen into either an open or a closed clubface position, swing back to the halfway position a few times, paying particular attention to swinging the hands back without rotation.

The other checkpoint for hand and arm rotation comes at the top of

The other checkpoint for hand and forearm rotation is the top of the swing. If you have swung back correctly, there will be more or less a straight line down the back of the left hand and the outside of the left forearm (A). If there is a convex angle between the back of the left hand and the outside of the left forearm, you have rotated the club into a closed position (B); if a concave angle, into an open position (C).

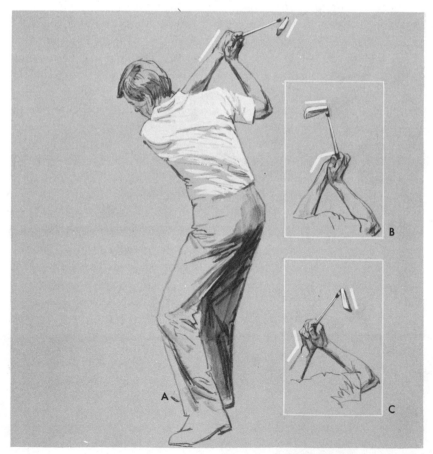

the swing. Swing to the top of the swing. If you have swung back without rotation, there will be more or less a straight line down the back of the left hand to the outside of the left forearm. If there is a concave angle between the back of the left hand and the outside of the left forearm, you have rotated the hands to the right, opening the clubface. If the back of the left hand and the outside of the left forearm make a convex angle, you have rotated the hands to the left, closing the clubface. If your hold on the club is as we have recommended, the toe of the club will point straight downward when the clubface is open, and the clubface will point directly at the sky when closed and will be in between these positions when there has been no rotation.

Where we have spoken of "open" and "closed" here, we have in each case described the extreme position, that is, fully open or fully closed. The particular positions you may have swung into may be "in between" positions; but if they are towards the open or closed positions, you can be sure that you have some rotation in your swing. Practice the "swing and stop" technique to the halfway back and top of the full swing positions until you can swing back with no unwanted rotation.

The "swing and stop" technique is also useful for checking to see that you are swinging on the right plane and maintaining the right plane. Here the checkpoints are the top of the swing and the finish of the swing. If you swing back to the top of the swing and your hands naturally swing to a point directly above the *right* shoulder, then in the follow-through they should swing through to a point above the *left* shoulder. If your swing is naturally more upright and you swing up to a point where your hands are closer to the neck, then your hands should swing through to a point where they are over a corresponding point closer to the neck. In other words, the position of the hands in relation to the right shoulder on the backswing should "mirror" the position of the hands in relation to the left shoulder in the follow-through.

If, however, you find that at the top of the swing your hands are outside the right shoulder rather than above it, you have swung back too far inside on what is known as too flat a swing plane. And if your hands swing through to a point outside the left shoulder, again the plane of the swing is too flat. In a similar fashion, if at the top of the swing your hands swing up to a point over or close to the neck, and in the follow-through to a point over or close to the neck, your swing is too upright. Sometimes you will find that you actually mix these faulty swing paths: You could swing up to a point outside the right shoulder and then through to a point inside the left shoulder, and so on.

In most cases these faulty swing paths are the result of leverage. The swing has a definite path, but, as we've said, you must allow the club to find its own natural path as a result of freely swinging the hands and club with the forearms and permitting the shoulders to turn in unison in response to the swing. Once you try to force the club into any particular path, you can count on trouble.

If you find that you have fallen into this error, you can straighten yourself out in a hurry by doing a stint of "non-stop" swings, paying particular attention to swinging back to the correct point for you in relation to the right shoulder and then through to the "mirror" position in relation to the left shoulder in the follow-through. Remember, the shorter and stockier you are, the more you will tend to swing up over the right shoulder and then through to over the left shoulder; the taller and more willowy you are, the more upright your swing will tend to be, and you will swing up and through to positions closer to the middle of the neck.

Another way of looking at the correct swing path versus faulty swing paths is suggested in something we often tell our pupils: A good golfer will always keep the club in front of himself. A bad golfer won't. To see how this works, take out your driver again and choke down on it, your right hand at the bottom of the grip. Set up to an imaginary ball in such a manner that the club is a foot or so off the ground. Notice the relationship of the club to your body: It is right in front of you—a line up the club shaft would point to the middle of your chest. If you keep that relationship during the backswing, you will swing the club up and down in the correct path.

A lot of golfers will move the club away in the backswing with the hands and arms only. In other words, they stop the body turn—and the shoulders in particular. If you do that one time, you'll notice that the club shaft is no longer in front of you. However, if you swing back as we've recommended with the shoulders responding correctly, the club shaft will remain in the same relationship to the middle of the chest. Swing to the halfway back position with the club shaft in front of you and from there you'll see that the arms can then swing on back to your correct slot at the top of the swing, whereas the "hands and arms only" swing will make you swing back outside the right shoulder and into a poor position.

The same sort of thing happens on the downswing. The force of the swing will turn the body and the club shaft will again be in front of you as you swing through the ball and on into the finish. Take a slow half-swing with the choked driver and you will see that the club goes through the ball and into the half-swing finish position with the club shaft maintaining its relationship to the middle of the chest.

Other Full-swing Exercises

Throughout this chapter we have been giving you many different ways in which to check on the quality of your swing. However, the most important thing is that you learn a true swinging action. Everything else is really secondary to that. Thus we have provided you with plenty of exercises and drills of various sorts so that you can learn the swing for yourself.

Here are four additional full-swing exercises that you can learn from. They may also be used as warm-up exercises before a round or as home exercises between rounds.

Exercise 1. Set up to an imaginary ball without a club. Extend the fingers of both hands so that the back of the left hand and the palm of the right face the target. The hands will be separate, with the right hand a little lower than the left. Now begin swinging your hands back and forth as in the "non-stop" swing, starting, say, at a half-swing back and through and working gradually up to a full swing. Make a conscious effort to swing the hands with the forearms, and allow the shoulders and legs to respond to the action.

You can learn much from this exercise. Note especially the weighted feel in the fingers and how the amount of shoulder turn and leg action is governed by the length of the arm swing. This is precisely the feel of a good swing. The hands are swung by the forearms—you don't consciously "do" anything with them at all. Notice how all parts of the body must work together; if you tried to force the action with the legs or the upper arms and shoulders, you would soon lose the swinging action. (Try it!) And this exercise punches home one of the points we have been making all along: The large muscles in the shoulders and upper arms and the leg muscles must take their orders from the swinging action, but if they ever get in charge of the action, you lose the swing.

Exercise 2. Set up to an imaginary ball, feet about 12 inches apart between the heels. The set is normal except for the way you position and hold the club. The club should be held horizontally in front of you with the hands grasping the shaft palms down and separated about shoulder width. Again swing back and forth, starting with the half-swing and working up to the full swing. This exercise is a great loosener of the golfing muscles; it also assures that the whole body works together in a unified, coordinated fashion.

Exercise 3. In a slight variation of Exercise 2, you grasp the shaft of the club with your hands a little farther apart on the shaft—say two feet apart this time—and you hold the shaft with the palms up. Swing back until the right arm points straight up in the air and then through until the left arm points straight up. This exercise will help your coordination and it will also *increase the flexibility of your shoulders,* ultimately enabling you to make a bigger shoulder turn. It is another fine warm-up exercise.

Exercise 4. This is the "non-stop" swing with the heavy club we mentioned earlier. While it obviously can help you with your swinging action, one stint a day of this exercise will gradually increase your flexibility so that you can make a larger shoulder turn. This exercise is the best way we know to strengthen your golf muscles.

Full Swings with Various Clubs

Now that you are comfortable making the full swing with the 7-iron, let's advance to the full swing with the other clubs. Actually, you have very little more to learn; the only adjustments you will have to

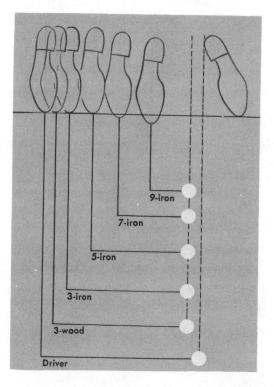

9-iron

7-iron

5-iron

3-iron

3-wood

Driver

Play the driver off the left heel. With fairway woods and irons, play the ball about a ball width to the right of the left heel. Progressively narrow the stance from the driver down to the short irons. From the 7-iron down through the wedges, progressively open the stance.

make are during the setup to the ball, and they are much the same as those we made as we advanced to the full swing.

As you progress from the 7-iron to the 5-iron and on to the longer clubs, the first adjustment you have to make is to take a slightly wider stance. As the club gets longer, so you make a bigger arc, and this results in more centrifugal force. Consequently, you must have a slightly wider foundation in order to keep your balance. You make this adjustment at the "feet together" phase of taking the set—simply move your right foot a little farther away to the right as you settle into your stance. When you use shorter clubs than the 7-iron (the 8, 9, or the wedges) you should narrow your stance a little by not taking the right foot away quite as much.

The main reason for narrowing the stance for the shorter clubs is that a wide stance is a power stance that gives you a forceful swing. You don't have the ability to finesse the swing, to be delicate with the swing. The clubs from the 5-iron to the 9-iron and the wedges are the scoring clubs; when we use them, we are trying to swing the club skillfully in order to hit the ball an exact distance. The clubs from the 4-iron through the woods are the power clubs; when we use them, we need the power and must widen the stance.

The width of the stance helps you control the power in the swing. With a wide stance, you have the foundation to support a more forceful swing. You can also make a more forceful arm swing. Thus you can obtain more windup in the legs going back and a more powerful release in the legs, especially the right knee, going through the shot. This leg action accentuates the speed of the arm swing. The increase in the lower body action also means there is more shifting of weight. The wider the stance, the more the body weight is set behind the ball initially and the more weight you have available to release through the ball. This in turn means that the arc of the driver, for example, is wider than that for the 7-iron. (The driver arc when viewed from the front is more elliptical than that of a 7-iron, which is pretty much a perfect circle in shape.)

The narrower stance used on the scoring clubs enables you to reduce the amount of leg drive in the shot. The narrower the stance, the more you make the action a pure arm swing with shoulder action. Since the arm swing, as we've said, controls the plane and the speed of the swing, this is why you can be more skillful and have more finesse from a narrower stance.

We recommend that you progressively open the stance from the 7-iron down through the wedges. This means that your shoulders will still be aligned parallel to the target line but that your feet and hips will be aligned progressively more to the left of the shoulders. The body, in the Obitz/Farley system, always times the blade into the ball, and the open stance enables you to release the right side to time the shot correctly from the narrower stance you adopt with these shorter clubs.

As regards the position of the ball for the various clubs, we recommend that you play the driver off the left heel, which for most people is the low point of the swing arc through the ball. With the driver, you want to catch the ball when the club is traveling parallel the ground, and playing the ball off the left heel will accomplish this purpose. Now, with the fairway woods and irons, you want to catch the ball with a slightly descending blow and nip the turf after the ball. To do this, you play the ball a little to the right of where you position the ball for the driver—a ball width to the right is roughly the correct amount.

We should point out, however, that the bottom of the swing arc is a point immediately below the left shoulder. If the golfer sets up to the ball as we recommended earlier, with the correct posture, shoulder and arm position then the bottom of the arc *has to be* at a point below the left shoulder because the left arm creates the arc of the swing. It is important for golfers to realize that the position of the left shoulder dictates the bottom of the swing arc. Take an extreme example—if a golfer adopted a super wide stance, similar to Doug Sanders', then obviously the low point of the swing will not be opposite the left heel, it might be three, four, or more inches to the right of the left heel. For most golfers, using the feet as a reference for the correct ball position is the easiest way, but it should be remembered that such recommendations do assume a stance of normal width.

The only other change you have to make as you move from the shorter clubs to the longer clubs is to alter what we call the "tilt" of the body—the angle the back makes with the ground when you view the golfer from the side looking down toward the target.

You may remember our saying that when you take your set you simply tilt forward from the hips, and that while you tilt forward with the upper body, you counterbalance yourself by allowing your seat to be pushed back slightly so that your weight remains balanced midway between the balls and heels of the feet. We now explain in more detail.

Whatever club you use, your arms will hang naturally from your shoulders. Yet the driver, for example, is not only longer than a short iron, but, when soled naturally, the grip end of the driver is higher off the ground than that of a short iron. Since your arms, obviously, are the same length whatever you do, the only means of adjustment is to alter the angle of "tilt."

The shorter the club in your hand, the more you have to tilt forward and counterbalance with your seat to the rear to keep your back in the desired straight position. The longer the club, the less the tilt necessary to get your hands to the right level, and the less you have to push your seat to the rear. (This adjustment of "tilt" is what makes the "Swing Center" slightly higher in the spine with longer clubs than with shorter clubs.)

The shorter the club, the more you have to tilt forward and counterbalance with your seat to the rear to get the hands to the required height and still maintain a straight back. The longer the club, the less the tilt and counter-balancing necessary. Here the "Tilts" for the driver and the 7-iron are demonstrated.

How do you tell if you have the right tilt for the club in your hands? By the position of your wrists. If your set is taken as we've recommended and there is the slight arching of the wrists we described earlier, then all is well. However, if you have to arch the wrists excessively, you have not tilted forward enough. If you have arched the wrists too much, you will have a tightness developing in the top of both wrists as you look down on them. And if you have to drop the hands so that there's an angle between the hands and the forearms, then you have tilted forward too much.

With a longer club like the driver, your hands will be slightly farther away from the body than for, say, a 7-iron. No, this is not a complication—it's just a natural move that we want you to understand fully. To demonstrate this for yourself, set up to an imaginary ball without a club, but take the correct set, say for a full 7-iron, including joining your hands together in a golfing hold on the imaginary handle. Now alter your tilt to that for a driver. You'll find that as your back rises, your hands go *forward* a little as a reflex. Now alter the tilt to the other end of the spectrum. Tilt forward for the setup for a mini-swing with the 7-iron, where you choke right down on the club. *Your hands have moved close to your legs.* However, if you analyze this, you were not conscious of altering the distance of the hands from the legs. *The correct tilt altered the hands' position for you.* Thus, if you allow your arms to hang from your shoulders naturally, as we've recommended, the hands will find their correct distance from the body by themselves because the correct tilt will put them there. Incidentally, this slight adjustment of the distance between the hands and the legs, together with the adjustment the tilt makes with regard to the height of the hands above the ground, is what enables you to compensate for the fact that the longer clubs set at a shallower angle or "lie" than the short clubs; it enables you to hold a driver or a 9-iron and still have the desired "arched" position of the hands.

The Swing Is the Same for All Clubs

As for differences in swinging the various clubs, there are virtually none. In learning the full swing for the 7-iron, you have, in effect, learned the full swing for every club in your bag. Now this is another advantage of learning the swing our way. When we advance our pupils from the 7-iron to the 5-iron to the 3-iron and then up the fairway woods to the driver, we make certain they realize that the swing is exactly the same with all clubs.

Whether you're thinking about the mechanics of the swing or about rhythm or tempo, you swing the short clubs the same as the long. (Many golfers learn the full swing with the wood first and for the rest of their golfing lives imagine that they have to put different swings on the other clubs.)

The common misconception of a high-handicap player is that the shorter clubs should be swung at a faster tempo than the longer ones—or that he should use a shorter swing on a short club than on a long club. Either of these thoughts will ruin the swing. The golfer who tries to swing at a faster tempo gets to jerking the club back and using leverage because he simply can't swing the club back that fast. (Remember, you can only swing the club so fast; if you try to swing it faster than your own individual speed of swing, you lose the swing.) When the average golfer tries to swing the club shorter, he usually falls into one of two errors: He either overuses the body and freezes the arms, wrists, and hands and pushes at the ball, or he doesn't allow the body to turn at all and gives it an arm and wrist flick. In neither case is this a true swinging action, and in neither case will the golfer get the results he seeks.

Whether you are making a full swing with a short iron, a medium iron, or a driver, the mechanics of the swing are the same, the tempo should be the same, and the rhythm should be the same. The photos of Dick Farley illustrate this: *He has swung just as fully on the wedge as for the driver, he has turned his shoulder and hips the same amount, there is the same cock of the wrists, and he has swung his hands up over the right shoulder in each case.* The only differences you can see are those necessitated by the different lengths and lies of the clubs themselves—the tilt, width of stance, and other matters we've already discussed. Even the fact that the wedge swing is more upright than that of the driver is not something that needs conscious thought; it is just something that is built in with the different lengths and lies of the clubs. You should never *think* of swinging one club on a flatter or more upright plane than another. All you have to do is stand correctly to the ball—and *swing it fully!*

Swinging the club fully is really the secret of developing the correct tempo for you. If you continually change the length of the swing for a normal full shot, you will never achieve consistency of tempo. As a general rule, the shorter the swing on a full shot, the faster your tempo becomes; the fuller you swing, the slower your tempo becomes.

As we said, tempo is individual; everyone can't swing back the same distance or at the same tempo. A thickset golfer like Harry Obitz will

A   B

Dick Farley demonstrates the full, normal swing with the wedge (A) and the driver (B). Note that he has swung just as fully with the wedge as with the driver.

have a full swing of only three-quarter length, whereas Dick Farley, who is tall and slim, will swing back past the horizontal. But Obitz is strong as a bull in the shoulders and arms, so he can swing faster than Farley, who is less muscular and needs to swing at a slower tempo. In both cases, however, the action is a swing and the arms are making the swing. Obitz gets his distance from a shorter, faster swing, Farley from a slower, longer swing.

If you practice swinging every club fully, you will soon find the correct tempo for you as an individual. And that correct tempo can be defined as the speed of swing that consistently gives you the greatest distance with each club. When you obtain consistent length you will find that you are not swinging with 100 percent of your strength. The figure is nearer 80 percent. That good tempo for you is the maximum speed at which you personally can still make a true, free swing. With anything above that, you run the risk of introducing leverage and slowing the speed of the club through the ball.

Obitz and Farley Say:

1. In learning the mini-swing or the quarter-swing, there's nothing more useful than the "brushing" technique.

2. Never "lean" on the club; just set it in the grass to acquire the correct "hanging" position.

3. The number one killer of the swing is a tight right-hand grip.

4. Always replay a good swing in your mind before hitting another ball. This mental image helps make your next swing a good one, too.

5. The "non-stop" swing gives you the time to learn and to ingrain the feels and characteristics of a true swing.

6. Learn to feel your "Swing Center"; it is one of the best tests that your swing is free and correct.

7. During a true swing, you will not be able to feel any sudden additional sideways pressure in the hands. If you do, you're not swinging.

8. If you're swinging well but striking the ball poorly, pay more attention to the ball and the target.

6

Advanced Course in the Swing

ONE OF THE DELIGHTS of golf is that there is never an end to the learning of it: There is never an end to perfecting your swing. That is why we decided to include the advanced course in the swing in this book. Over the years we have trained more than 100 golf professionals to appear with us in our "Swing's the Thing" golf show, so this is not a case of "do what we say," but one of "do as we do!"

The "Feet Together" Swing

Truly one of the greatest aids that we know for learning the true swing is the "feet together" swing. When you're standing with your feet apart in a normal setup position it's all too easy to try to force the swing. As you know now, this results in leverage and trying to "muscle" the ball with the big muscles in the upper arms and shoulders or the legs. *The "feet together" swing prevents this from happening.* If you try to "muscle" the ball with the upper arms and shoulders, or if you try to force the swing with conscious leg action, you simply lose your balance and fall over! The same thing happens if you try to jerk the club back, pick it up, swing too fast, or use any of the other wrong ways to move a golf club.

As a result you learn speedily that the only way to move the club effectively is with a true, free swinging action. You are forced to swing back with the forearms swinging the club and the shoulders and legs merely responding to the action. After a while you will amaze yourself by how *easily* you are swinging and yet how *fast* your hands and arms and the club are whipping through the impact area. *It's as though your arms, your hands, and the club were a flail and your shoulders and legs were only permitting the flail to function.*

You'll also learn that a true swing, a free swinging action, enables you to keep your balance during the golf stroke. The true swing keeps you centered; it is leverage that throws you off balance. In fact, we'll say this: Any time you lose your balance while doing the "feet together" swing, you've used some sort of improper action.

Soon you will begin to feel that the golf swing is an easy and graceful thing and that distance comes as much from the timing of the swing as from the force of it. In some ways, that's the most important lesson of all.

Every golfer should work up to hitting balls with the feet together. You should start without a ball with the quarter- and half-swings and then work your way up to full swings. Once you've gotten the hang of it in these "dry runs," repeat the procedure hitting balls.

As for the club to begin with, you can't do better than the 5-iron; it's the ideal, all-round practice club. It has enough length so that you get to swing it fully and yet you don't have to swing it hard. And it has enough loft so that getting the ball into the air is not a factor. If you're a beginner, we suggest you start off with a 7-iron for just a touch more confidence, and then graduate to the 5-iron as soon as you feel you're ready. (For all the shots described in this chapter, use the 5-iron to begin with, except as otherwise noted.)

By the way, there's nothing better than the "feet together" swing for getting your swing back in a hurry after a layoff. We remember one time in the early 1960s, when we had the Montauk Golf Club for the summer season, playing in a friendly fivesome one evening with professionals Mil Radler and Rick McCord and Desmond Tolhurst, who was down from New York to interview us for some articles for Golf Magazine. This was the first time Desmond had worked with us, so he wasn't familiar with our ideas on the golf swing.

Dick Farley teed it up on the first hole, a par 4, and—much to Desmond's obvious surprise—took his set with the feet together and then smoothed it down the middle *without ever spreading his feet apart!* Desmond's face was a picture as Dick played hole after hole, in par or better, with his feet together. Eventually, Desmond asked the inevitable question: "What the —— are you doing?"

Dick's reply was simply, "I haven't been able to play for the last week, and this is how I get back my rhythm, timing, and balance."

If you still can't quite believe the importance of the "feet together" swing and what it can do for your game, we'd like to tell you what our old friend Jimmy Thomson once told us.

"When I was a youngster," Jimmy said, "I wasn't very big. When my family came over from North Berwick, Scotland, my father became the pro at the Country Club of Virginia, and I caddied and helped around the shop. I was always the short hitter among the other kids, so I asked my dad for some help. His theory on long hitting was based on one thing—balance. *If you have perfect balance at impact you can swing that much harder; you can get really fast hand action.* (Our italics.)

"My dad simply stuck a short iron into my hand and told me to hit balls with my feet together. I stuck at it day after day, and I remember how proud I was when he finally decided I had learned the golf swing. He put a driver in my hand with these words, 'That's it, Jimmy. Now you can outdrive anybody.'"

How right he was. Although Jimmy was never a giant physically— in his prime he was 5' 10" and weighed 188 pounds—he gave the ball a ride the likes of which we've never seen. When he won the North American driving championship at the General Brock tournament in 1938, his 10 drives averaged 324 yards. His longest was a clout of 386 yards!

We hope this has given you an idea of the value of the "feet together" swing; if there is such a thing as a shortcut to improving your swing, this is it. For the most important point you have to learn is that *75 percent of the golf swing is in the arm swing and in the response of the shoulders to the arm swing.* And the "feet together" swing will demonstrate this most effectively because with the feet together you have to swing mostly with the arms. By taking a large portion of the leg action out of the shot, the "feet together" swing puts you in an ideal position to learn this vital 75 percent of the golf swing in isolation. Once you have mastered that, it is a relatively simple matter to learn how to time the action of the legs with the basic movement.

Make no mistake about this: We *do* contradict the commonly held proposition that you get your power from sliding your hips or driving your legs. You don't. You'll find that you can get to within 10 or 15 yards of your own best distance with a 5-iron when you stand with your feet together. Your legs help you time the swing, and they do contribute some power, *but the majority of the power comes from the arm swing in coordination with the shoulder action.*

The "One Foot" Swing

Most of you will have thought that swinging balanced on one foot is merely a trick shot that you shouldn't attempt. We disagree. We don't say this is for beginners, but, when you've developed a pretty good swing and can execute the "feet together" swing without too much difficulty, you should graduate to the "one foot" swing. It can teach you something about the true swing because you can't swing freely and

Harry Obitz demonstrates the "one-footer."

properly unless you have good balance—and this swing is the sternest test of balance we know.

You should begin your practice in the same general way as that for the "feet together" swing: Start with the quarter-swing with the 5-iron and work up to the full swing. Take plenty of practice swings before attempting to hit a ball. When hitting balls, position the ball off the middle of the left foot if playing the "left foot only" shot and off the middle of the right foot if playing the "right foot only" shot.

When you first attempt this swing, instead of standing with all your weight on the left foot with the right foot completely off the ground, begin by placing your right foot behind you so that the toe just rests on the ground. In other words, although you have 95 percent of your weight on the left foot, you'll put a little weight on the right foot so that you have some help initially in learning the shot. As you perfect the "one foot" shot, you can progress to raising the right foot completely off the ground.

Do the same thing when learning the "one foot" swing on the right foot: Rest the toe of the left foot on the ground until you can graduate to raising the left foot completely off the ground.

In many ways the "one foot" swing exaggerates the effect you experienced with the "feet together" shot. You might get away with just a *hint* of leverage in the "feet together" swing, but you won't get away with it when playing off one foot! With anything other than a pure swinging action, you will topple over. In learning the "one foot" swing, you will truly be taking the perfecting of your swing one step further.

Another important thing to be learned from the "one foot" shot is the necessary responding action in the shoulders to the arm swing. When you stand on the left foot you will find that, in order to maintain your balance, your right shoulder must turn out of the way immediately on the backswing. If you don't, you'll fall over. When you stand on the right foot, it teaches you that, as you come through the ball, the left shoulder must come up to let the right side go down and through.

How far can you take the "one foot" swing? Leo Diegel, the PGA Champion of 1928 and 1929, scored in the 70s when playing rounds off one foot! No, we're not suggesting that you actually play rounds this way yourself, but mastering the "one foot" shots gives a new perspective on the swing—in more ways than one, as Harry Obitz can tell you.

Harry Obitz: The first time I was exposed to the "one-footer" was when I went with Joe Kirkwood at Huntingdon Valley near Philadelphia back in

1938. Leo Diegel was close by at Philmont and I used to go over to his place and practice. I saw Leo practicing the "one foot" shot and making money out of it. Here's what he would do.

Leo used to play matches against 86-shooters, knowing that he could shoot better than 80 off one foot. He usually shot 76 to 78 off one foot, but he used 80 as his number for betting purposes. So they go out and play, and Leo trims the guy on the front nine playing off the right foot. But Leo says, "I don't want to take your money, so I'll play the back nine off the left foot." Now the guy has to go along, and again Leo chills him 3 and 2, no trouble at all.

At this point, Leo applies the cruncher. "I'll tell you what I'll do," he'd say, "I'll play you the rest of the way with my feet crossed!" Well, again the guy has to go for it. He owes Leo at this point, say $100, so he says, "Okay, I'll bet you another $100 you can't do that." And Leo cools the guy 1 up and he's made $200. He used to do that all the time.

Harry Obitz makes the "crossed feet" swing.

In practicing the "one-footer" myself, I soon learned that it didn't make a lot of difference whether you played with your feet together, off one foot, or with crossed feet. It didn't affect the heart of the golf swing, which is that the arms make the swing. I also found that as long as you had the arm swing, and the turn of the shoulders that went with the arm swing, you could make a swing and get almost as much distance as with both feet spread normally. You would lose a little distance because you had, so to speak, cut the legs out of it, but that was all.

Dick Farley and I have trained some professionals for our show, who when they came to us used a lot of leverage and were just "beaters" of the ball. So we'd throw them the "one-footer" and they'd have a terrible time, falling down all over the place! And they did that until they learned that "the Swing's the Thing." Then they amazed themselves that it could be that easy. What's more, they found that they could get far more distance with a swinging action than they ever did leveraging the club.

If you learn to swing off one foot, you will find it pretty simple in contrast to swing with both feet on the ground, both in maintaining correct balance in motion and in proper coordination of the shoulders with the arm swinging action. You will learn that it is the correct action of the shoulders responding to the swing that is responsible for keeping you centered over the ball as you swing.

The "Bare Foot" Shot

For our thoughts about playing in bare feet, we owe a debt to our old friend Sam Snead. We've known him for years and have often had the distinct pleasure of hearing Sam regale a group with stories that are always hilarious—if not always printable! This one is not only printable, it's instructive and amusing as well.

In 1942, Sam was at the Masters tournament chatting with sportswriters when Fred Corcoran came by. Always one to promote Sam, Fred claimed that Sam could throw away his shoes and beat the field playing in his bare dogs. The writers thought this was going too far and frankly didn't believe it—not knowing that Sam, of course, had grown up playing in his bare feet and in fact found it difficult at first to play in golf shoes!

To cut a long story short, Sam kicked off his shoes, birdied the first two holes, and eventually finished the round with a fine 68!

The point of the story is that playing in bare feet prevents you from hitting too hard. If you do hit too hard, you lose your balance. If you're a golfer who suffers from trying to swing too fast or hit too hard (in our book, leveraging the club rather than swinging it), a spell of practicing where you kick off your golf shoes can really help. You'll find that you are forced to cut back the speed of the swing to the point where you can handle it, to the point where you are no longer leveraging the club. That's your ideal tempo for this stage in your development.

Playing "bare foot" shots can help in other ways, too. It can help you to get a much finer feel of the correct inward set of the legs at address. Without shoe leather intervening between the feet and the ground, you can really get the feel of having the weight set on the insides of the feet at the setup position—a feel that will carry over when you play shots normally with shoes on. You can also use the "bare foot" shot to help you appreciate all we've said about correct weight transference and good balance in motion during the swing, either with normal shots or the ones discussed in this section. It gives you a heightened awareness of these things that, again, carries over into your regular golf.

Perhaps you are hesitant to discover for yourself the value of "bare foot" shots. "Sam Snead grew up playing that way," we hear you say, "but you wouldn't catch me playing in bare feet! I would be laughed off the course."

All right, we'll draw the line at bare feet! But let us make a case for stockinged feet, at least. When we were preparing this section of the book, our Boswell (Desmond Tolhurst) told us a story that should remove any hesitancy you may have.

Desmond and his father were in England, playing a round at a course away from home. It was midsummer and the course was so dry the fairways were hard as concrete. (The British don't irrigate fairways as we do.) British golfers are usually prepared for these conditions; they carry, in addition to regular spiked shoes, an extra pair of "summer" shoes with specially designed rubber soles. This day, however, Desmond's Father had left his "summer" shoes at home and decided to play in street shoes.

The results were disastrous. If Tolhurst Père had a fault in golf, it was a tendency to try and hit the daylights out of the ball rather than swing the club freely! This tendency, plus the fact that he was "skating" on top of the hard ground, meant a succession of missed shots. After a couple of holes, thoroughly exasperated, Desmond Senior kicked off his golf shoes and announced, "Well, I couldn't play much worse in my stockinged feet!"

In fact, he played magnificently from that point on. As Des told us, *his father was forced to swing truly on every shot or else lose his* balance. The result was a fine 80 for the round, some 5 to 8 shots better than his average score!

Moral: We hope you don't have to play in stockinged feet, but we trust you will practice this way when you need this medicine—you can do your golf swing nothing but good.

The "Closed Eyes" Shot

We introduced the idea of swinging with the eyes closed as a way of intensifying your feel of the swing in order to feel your "Swing Center." It has other uses too; it can provide a breakthrough for some people.

We once had a pupil who learned to swing pretty well in our "dry run" procedures, including "brushing" and the "non-stop swing," prior to actually hitting the ball. But when confronted with a ball, all too often he would resort to some form of leverage to move the club. One day, having asked him to take some "closed eyes" practice swings in which he swung beautifully, we decided on this procedure:

We had him set up to a ball with a middle iron, and, without warning him in advance, told him to close his eyes and swing. The result was all we—or he—could have wished for: A fine, free swing, the ball going straight out for good distance. We repeated this at regular intervals until he was convinced that he didn't have to hit the ball, that all he had to do was swing freely, and that it was the free swing that caught the ball and sent it to the target. Once this breakthrough was made, progress was rapid and he got to a single figure handicap the same season.

In hitting balls with the "closed eyes" swing, we suggest you start out with the quarter-swing and graduate yourself to the half-, the three-quarter, and the full swing as you feel you have perfected each one. In this way, you will learn much about the true swing, for closing your eyes intensifies the primary feel of the swing—the forearms swinging the hands and club. You will also become more aware of the fact that the big muscles of the body in the upper arms and shoulders, and those in the legs, must respond to but not lead the swinging action in the forearms and hands. If the big muscles are allowed to dominate, this short-circuits the swing and you miss the ball.

In our "Swing's the Thing" show, we use a variation of the "closed eyes" shot which we call the "blindie." Here you set up to the ball, lift your head, and, instead of looking at the ball, look straight ahead and make the swing.

The "closed eyes" shot and the "blindie" teach you (besides the obvious, that "the Swing's the Thing") that once you've set the "tilt" of the body at address (the angle the back makes with the ground when you look down toward the target at the golfer), you must retain that "tilt" throughout the swing. If you retain the "tilt," the club will swing right back to the ball; if you raise or lower the "tilt," you'll miss it. It also proves the importance of establishing the right "tilt" in the set. If you don't, you will probably raise or lower the "tilt" during the swing, and again you'll miss the ball.

"One Hand" Shots

One of the supreme challenges of learning golf is that in the true swing both sides of the body must function equally efficiently. If we were called on to specify the key physical attribute of the ideal pupil— one who would learn a free swinging action quickly—we'd have to say that attribute is ambidexterity.

It is no coincidence that many of the greatest golfers have been ambidextrous—among them, Bobby Jones, Walter Hagen, "Long Jim" Barnes, and our old friend Joe Kirkwood, the trick-shot artist par excellence. Harry Vardon, still the only man to have won six British Opens, was also ambidextrous. The story goes that, as a professional at the Ganton club in England, he got tired of giving his members impossible odds in matches and beating them. Harry's solution was to outfit himself with a set of left-handed clubs. He then conceded handicap strokes to the members, rating himself as scratch. But it made no difference— he still won all the matches!

How does that affect me? you ask. I can't help being right-handed (or left-handed, as the case may be). Yes, you *can;* that's the whole point. And you do it by practicing "one hand" shots.

Let's trace the career of a typical adult taking up the game. The pupil is right-handed and plays with right-handed clubs. His first efforts at swinging at a golf ball will invariably be almost totally dominated by the right side. If left to himself, he will do any one or more of the following: Pick up the club with his right hand, allow his left arm to start in a bent position and bend more during the swing, try to pressure the club with the strong muscles in his right upper arm and shoulder, and so on. In desperation, he goes to a golf professional. The pro sees there's no left-side action in this pupil's motion at all. So he first gets the pupil to stand in a decent position at the ball, extending the left arm and setting the right arm in toward the side in a "soft" position. Now the professional tells the pupil to do everything with his left side, to keep the left arm straight, to turn the left shoulder under the chin, and so on—he insists that the pupil do nothing with the right side at all.

This approach is wrong for several reasons: First, the pro asks the pupil to relate everything to the *left* side when the pupil may well have done nothing, athletically speaking, with the left side in his life! Worse, even if the pupil perseveres with such a method, he or she will develop a one-sided swing. It may even look quite pretty, but it will be powerless *because both sides of the body are not being used.*

Most golfers, even great golfers, start off life with a dominant side. Jack Nicklaus, for example, is right-handed. But all great golfers, including Jack, overcome this initial handicap by developing the action in their "weak" side to the point where they are virtually ambidextrous, at least with regard to executing the golf swing.

This is the method we favor. It won't do to tell a right-handed person to stop using the right side and do everything with the left side. We advocate *building up the left side to do its proper job.* And the way to do it is with single-handed swings.

To begin your work with "one hand" shots, start with some practice swings with a 7-iron. Take the club in your left hand, choke well down on the grip, and swing the club in a quarter-swing back and through. Repeat about 10 times. Then advance to the half-swing, holding the club a little higher on the grip. Again, repeat 10 times. Continue with the three-quarter and full swings in similar fashion. Then use the same procedure with the right hand.

We suggest you start with practice swings rather than by making shots with a ball because, frankly, even quite good golfers find it difficult to make single-handed swings, especially with their "weak" side. As for the high-handicapper (above a 12 handicap for a man or a 16 for a woman), if we had suggested their hitting balls initially with either hand, their swings would have been so shaky that they would have been discouraged.

This is the last thing we want to happen. One-handed swings are so good for your swing, and you can learn so much just from practice swings with either hand, that we don't want you to abandon them if they don't seem to be for you at first. They are for you, but on an individual basis. If you're a beginner and strongly right-handed, you may well find the left-handed swing extremely difficult to start with. If this is the case, keep on making quarter-swings until you can execute them with ease, and only advance to the longer swings when you're really ready. If you're a low-handicapper, then obviously you can advance more quickly; even so, you may find a rude shock initially with your "weak" side. If so, that's exactly what you should find out about your swing—*it may be the very thing that has been holding back your progress!* If you're in-between in ability, then use your own good common sense about advancing to the longer swings.

One of the most important things you can learn from one-handed swings is the individual pressure with which you should hold with each hand. If you hold firmly with your left hand, you will find that your left side will react nicely to the left-hand swing. However, if you hold too tightly with the right hand, you will find it impossible to get a swinging action going with the right-hand swing. This experience will teach you exactly how firmly to hold each hand; the proper blending will make for a good hold and a good feel in the regular two-handed swing.

When you make the left-hand swing, you will appreciate what we said about the left arm staying extended to create and maintain the radius of the swing; you will be able to feel the backhand swing that the left side makes. In the right-hand swing you will appreciate how the right arm must wind up as though making an underhand throw—it must bend at the elbow going back and then release into a straight position in the follow-through, just as if you were throwing a ball.

Other points you'll appreciate concern the roles of the hands, the arms, the shoulders, and the lower body. You'll find that if you only use hand action, you'll end up just twisting the club with the hands. Even on the mini-swing you need some arm swing—and a little responding movement from the shoulders and legs. As for the hands, you'll be convinced that they're not the activating force of the swing, that they just hold the club in position during the swing.

You are going to find, of course, that one side of your body is much less adept than the other (unless you're lucky enough to be naturally ambidextrous!). Decide now that you will give your "weak" side twice as much practice as the other. But don't neglect your "strong" side. Many pupils have difficulty with their "strong" side, especially when this is the right side (as it usually is), and particularly on the longer swings, where you appreciate what your left side usually does for you by its absence! The right arm has a tendency to fly away from the body on a full swing, but with practice this can be controlled; the secret is in *learning the wind-up action of the right arm*, which bends the arm at the elbow and keeps it in correct position. If you have difficulty, practice a few imaginary underarm throws to get the feel of this.

When do you graduate to hitting balls with "one hand" swings? Again, the answer is individual. Low-handicap players can proceed to this after a few minutes of practice swinging. Beginners and high-handicappers might not be ready for months. But whatever stage you're at, don't neglect "one hand" swings. They provide a marvelous education in the true swing, they train both sides of the body to their individual roles in the swing, and they strengthen the golfing muscles with the best possible exercise—the golf swing itself.

One last point about one-handed swings: To build up a strong golf swing, there's nothing better than one-handed "non-stop" swinging with a heavy club—either the lead-tape creation we talked of earlier or a sand wedge—in combination with "non-stop" swinging with the normal two-handed hold. A few minutes a day of this exercise can work wonders for your swing.

"Lift and Lift" Shot

This could be described as the ultimate "one foot only" shot, because what you do is this: You start in a normal golf set with the 5-iron, both feet on the ground and spread the normal distance apart, but halfway back you lift your left foot off the ground and complete your backswing on the right foot. To swing down, you place your left foot back on the ground, and at about impact you start to lift your right foot off the ground, finishing the swing with your weight all on the left foot and the right foot up in the air.

We must admit that it requires an almost perfect swing to hit balls with the "lift and lift" shot. However, as an exercise it has great value because one of the most common faults of the average golfer is to *slide* the weight from the left foot to the right in the backswing. And he does this lateral swaying action in the fond belief that he is shifting his weight correctly. The term "weight shift" is really a misnomer. The weight moves through the feet during the swing, as we have seen, so that at the top of the backswing you feel the weight on the inside and back of the right foot and, in the follow-through, you feel the weight on the outside and back of the left foot. But what causes this movement of the weight is not a lateral shifting action: *it is the upswing of the arms and the club in concert with the shoulder turn that causes any weight transference that takes place.*

The "lift and lift" shot really gives you the feel of the right weight transference. As you swing back, lifting your left foot, you will exaggerate slightly the correct feel you should have in the normal swing of the weight moving toward the back and inside of the right foot. In the downswing you will have the correct feel of the weight being on the outside and back portion of the left foot, again a slight exaggeration of what you would normally feel.

In learning the "lift and lift" swing, you have to break it down into two movements. Swing back, lift your left foot off the ground, complete the upswing of the arms and club and the shoulder turn, and hold that position for a moment. Then put your left foot down on the ground, swing down and then up into the finish, lifting your right foot off the ground, and hold the finish for a moment. Do this for as many times as it takes to get the feel of the movement, and then try to blend the two into one flowing movment.

As with all of these advanced swings, you will find that the "lift and lift" shot is a ruthless exposer of faulty motions during the shot. Only a free swinging motion will do the job.

The "Rainbow" Shot

One of the most impressive trick shots is one in which you line up a dozen or so balls some six inches apart in a row in front of you and then go down the row hitting the balls in quick succession. It's even more impressive if you do it turning your face away from the ball, as Joe Kirkwood used to do, or swinging alternately at the balls with a left-hand only swing and then a right-hand only swing, as Paul Hahn used to do so effortlessly! We're not suggesting you emulate Joe or Paul right away (though there's no reason why you shouldn't graduate to it if you wish), but we do recommend a simplified version, which goes like this:

Line up a dozen balls in a row, as described above. Set up to the first ball, looking at the ball normally, and make a half-swing, hitting the ball. As you make your follow-through, your right heel will be up and your weight on the left foot, so it's easy to step forward with your right foot to set up to the next ball. Once your right foot is in position, it's easy to move the left foot up beside it and swing the club back behind the next ball. Make another half-swing and repeat the action down the line. After a while you'll find yourself settling into a rhythm that goes like this: Swing back, swing through; right foot forward, left foot forward, set club behind next ball; swing back, and so on. That rhythm and tempo is what we're after.

In many ways this "row of balls" shot is almost like "non-stop" swinging, but here you are hitting balls. It does give you much the same benefits: You strike the ideal tempo for you and you fall into a natural rhythm of taking your set and swinging that enhances your regular game.

When you become adept at this first version, you can take the shot a stage further: Hit the first ball as you did before but, instead of stopping to address the second ball, make your next backswing while stepping forward with the right foot and swing through while stepping in with your left foot. So the rhythm now is: Right foot, backswing, left foot, downswing, and so on.

This is truly a "non-stop" swing hitting balls and a marvelous aid in developing both the ideal tempo for your swing and the rhythm that suits you individually. It goes without saying that only a free swinging action will enable you to keep going down the row of balls without a hitch.

There are two other important points that are literally driven home by the "rainbow" shot in its final form. The first is the proper weight transference: As you swing back, your weight is planted on your right foot, as it should be. When you swing through, your weight has to be planted on your left foot, as it should be (otherwise you can't step forward with your right foot and swing on back again). *You are literally forced to transfer your weight correctly.*

The second thing you learn from the "rainbow" shot is the proper reaction of the body to the arm swing. It will again emphasize the importance of establishing and retaining the correct "tilt," which in turn will help you make the good arm swing and shoulder turn. But where you'll really feel the action in this shot is in the feet and legs. You'll find that you don't "dance" on your feet. You have to keep them pretty close to the ground and in position to react to the swing rather than lead it. You'll find out how the knees work: You can't be ducking them up and down; they have to stay on a level throughout the action. Your hips also have to stay on the same level they started on, and you'll learn that they do not make a big, roundabout leading action, but merely respond to the swing.

"Building the Swing"

Throughout this chapter we've been punching home our credo that the arms make the swing and the body times the swing. We've given you plenty with which to develop a fine arm swing, and now here is the best way we know to learn how to blend the complete body action with the arm swing.

As a warm-up, take the 5-iron and set up with a normal stance. The action is a continuous back and forth action like the "non-stop" swing. To begin, swing the club back and forth with a little quarter-swing.

Then swing a little farther back with the arms into the half-swing and through to the half-swing finish; then go to the three-quarter swing and then the full swing.

You will find that the farther back you swing your arms, the more your shoulders will respond and turn until on the full swing they're fully wound up. Similarly, you'll learn that you need a little response from the legs in the quarter-swing but a much larger response in the full swing. And by continually swinging back and forth rhythmically, you'll also learn how the leg and shoulder action times the blade through the ball.

Once you have the feel of this, you can take it a step farther (this is another shot we did in our show): Put down 8 balls in a row. Maintaining the same tempo throughout, hit the first ball with a quarter-swing, the second ball with a half-swing, the third with a three-quarter swing, the fourth with a full swing. Then reverse the process. Hit the fifth ball with the full swing and work down to the quarter-swing with the last three balls.

This series of shots teaches you to use the same rhythm and tempo when you make a quarter-swing as when you make a full swing; what gives you the distance primarily is the length of the swing, not the tempo. Naturally, when you make the full swing, there's more turn of the shoulders, more coil/recoil, and thus more club speed through impact. But the tempo with which you swing should be the same, even though you're getting higher club speed through the ball.

It is important to realize that you should not attempt to get distance out of a short swing at a fast tempo. What "building the swing" does is to make you recognize that the longer you swing the club, the greater the centrifugal force (and the more distance) you develop.

Just as important as the tempo, "building the swing" teaches that the arm swing and body action are a blend, and, if you do enough of this practice, you will learn to coordinate your body with whatever length of arm swing you make.

The "Pendulum" Swing

Many teachers have talked about the value of the forward press, but none of them has given an explanation of it to our satisfaction. The "pendulum" swing will show you what we mean.

Set up to the ball but, instead of soling the club in the grass behind the ball, set the club half an inch above the ball. Then swing your arms forward a foot or so, releasing the right leg a little as you do, pause, and swing back to the top of the swing and swing through, catching the ball on the downswing as usual.

The value of the forward press is the same, in miniature, as that of practicing the "pendulum" swing. It gives you the feel of how arms and body will blend when they pass through the ball as you make your move forward, the arms swinging through and the right side releasing. On the reaction backward it gives you the feel of how the arms swing away from the ball with the body responding. All of this adds to the truisms that, first, it is easier to start from a slight recoil action and, second, it is necessary to break up any tension that may have accumulated in the set.

In addition to helping you understand the value of a forward press, the "pendulum" swing also gives you a fine feel of "swing." It is well worth practicing on its own merits.

The "Slow Motion" Swing

This type of swing, in which the golfer swings back and through in ultra-slow motion, has been a staple of exhibitions, clinics, and trick-shot shows over the years. Yet we know of no teacher who has recommended this practice to his or her pupils. This is a peculiar lapse. In order to make a good "slow motion" swing, you have to know how to make a true swing—and until you can make a good "slow motion" swing, you don't really understand "swing."

Harry Obitz remembers the first time he saw someone practice the slow motion swing this way.

Harry Obitz: The first guy I saw actually make a good "slow motion" swing, who was not doing it just as a trick but was actually working with it, was Johnny Dawson. He was the uncrowned king of the amateurs back in the middle and late 1930s. He worked for Spalding on the public relations side of the business and traveled all over for them. Because of his connection with Spalding he was denied entry into the U.S. Amateur, but he won a lot of tournaments both pro and amateur. When I saw him actually *practicing* the "slow motion" shot, it was as if a light went on in my head. I went out immediately to the practice ground to do it myself.

The "slow motion" swing, I found, has two valuable properties. Because it's slow, you have the time to study the action which you never have on a normal swing. You can find out what you're doing right and you can spot your errors much more easily. As I continued practicing the "slow motion" swing, I found that it had the property of impressing the right moves on the subconscious mind—your muscle memory, if you like. I began immediately to teach it to all my pupils, and later it became a part of the Obitz/Farley system.

Since that time, I've found that all fine swingers of a golf club can execute a good "slow motion" swing. Jimmy Thomson, the long hitter, was one. Jimmy used to put on the "slow motion" swing at the clinics they gave before every PGA tour event in those days. Jimmy, of course, was a fine swinger; unless you were, you couldn't hit the ball as far as he did. On the other hand, I can't think of one golfer who had a bad swing and could make a good "slow motion" swing. The two just don't go together.

We think you should practice all aspects of the swing in slow motion. Practice the "brushing" motion this way, and practice everything from the quarter-swing to the full swing. You will find it a marvelous self-diagnostic tool—as well as a refreshingly different medium through which to learn the swing.

In this advanced course in learning the swing, we've described fully all those shots that are of prime importance in developing and perfecting your swing. Of course, there are other "shots." One of our particular favorites is one Harry does, the "sitting in the chair" shot.

Harry Obitz executes the "Sitting in the Chair" shot.

Harry does this with a driver or a putter; depending on conditions, he can get 225 to 240 yards with a driver and up to 200 yards with a putter. Although Harry has practiced the shot for some 30 years (along with all the others we've described), it is not a shot you should feel obliged to practice. What it does prove is that the "Swing's the Thing," even when the golfer is sitting in a chair. (The arms make at least 75 percent of the swing, but you still need the body, including the legs, to time the swing even when perched on the edge of a chair.)

Obitz and Farley Say:

1. To learn the arm swing and the responding action of the shoulders, there's nothing better than the "feet together" swing and the "one foot" swing.

2. To stop yourself from overpowering the swing, kick off your shoes!

3. To break yourself of the leverage habit, close your eyes!

4. "One hand" swings teach both sides of the body to do their job.

5. Until you can make the "slow motion" swing, you don't truly understand "swing."

7

Understanding the Flight
of the Ball

THE GREATEST PROBLEM with golfers today (and indeed with teaching the game) is that two important factors are not fully understood. The first is: How do you swing? We believe we've covered that aspect of golf thoroughly in the preceding six chapters. The second factor, equally important, is this: What makes the ball react the way it does—why does it fly straight toward the target or to the left or right of it, why does it curve, and what makes the ball fly high or low?

We'll attack this second problem in two parts. First, we'll explain the mechanics of the club and the ball—what happens at impact that makes the ball behave the way it does. Second, we'll give you the means whereby you can analyze the flight of the ball and determine how to correct undesirable flights (hooks, slices, too high, too low, and so on).

The Straight Ball—and Others

A golf ball flies in a certain pattern not by chance but because of two factors: the path of the swing through impact and the direction in which the clubface is aimed at impact. For a ball to fly straight, the path of the swing through impact must be as we have taught you, from inside the target line before impact to square at impact to inside the target line after impact, and the clubface must be square to the target line at impact. Any other swing path or clubface alignment will result in something other than a straight shot to the target.

If a ball is pulled (flies straight to the left), the path of the swing was more from outside the target line before impact to inside the target line after impact than the correct inside-to-square-to-inside swing path. And the reason the ball flew straight to the left rather than curving is that the clubface was exactly square to this faulty swing path at impact. If a ball is pushed (flies straight to the right), the opposite applies: The path of the swing was too much from the inside toward the outside and, again, the clubface was exactly square to this faulty swing path at impact.

A slice (curve to the right) or a hook (curve to the left) occurs because the clubface at impact is respectively open or closed in relation to the swing path. If the clubface is open, the clubface imparts clockwise spin to the ball (looking from a position directly above the ball at impact) and the ball curves to the right. If the clubface is closed, counter-clockwise spin has been imparted to the ball, curving it to the left.

In the case of either the slice or the hook, there can be only three basic variations.

Slice:

1. The ball starts to the left of the target line, then curves to the right.
2. The ball starts straight, then curves to the right.
3. The ball starts to the right of the target line and curves farther to the right.

Hook:

1. The ball starts to the right of the target line, then curves to the left.
2. The ball starts straight, then curves to the left.
3. The ball starts to the left of the target line and curves farther to the left.

Correcting the Curve Balls

To correct a sliced or a hooked flight, you have to straighten out the curve first, then correct any deviation to the left or right of target. If, for example, your ball is starting to the right and slicing farther to the right, you must first get rid of the slice so that you are hitting straight to the right. After that it becomes a comparatively simple matter to correct the swing so that the ball flies straight to the target. If

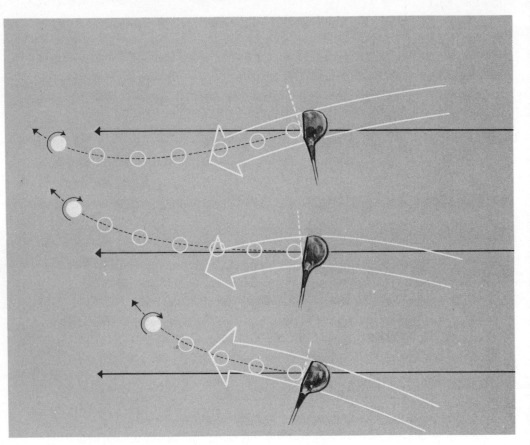

Slice (Type 1). Ball starts to left of target line, then curves back to right.
Slice (Type 2). Ball starts straight, then curves to right.
Slice (Type 3). Ball starts to the right of target line, then curves farther to right.

your initial move is to try to compensate for the ball finishing to the right or left of target—and this is typically what the average golfer attempts to do—you merely compound the problem.

Let's suppose the ball starts a little to the right of the target line and then, at the end of its flight, slices to the right and finishes in the right rough. The golfer sees where the ball has finished and his first move is to try to make the ball fly more to the left. So he alters his set-up so that his body is aligned to the left of target and, for good measure, he tries to pull the ball to the left. His state is now worse than it was.

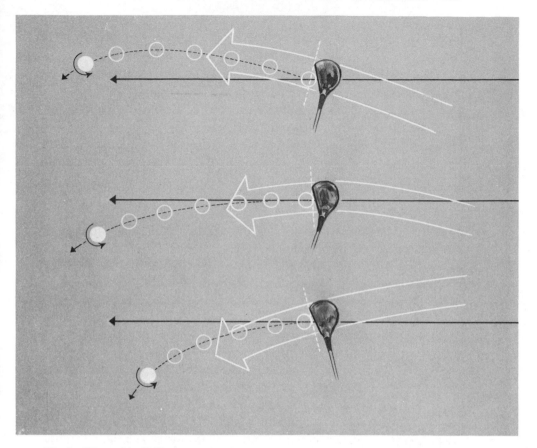

Hook (Type 1). Ball starts to right of target line, then curves to left.
Hook (Type 2). Ball starts straight, then curves to left.
Hook (Type 3). Ball starts to left of target line, then curves farther to left.

The path of the swing will now be more to the left, but the clubface will be more open in relation to that swing path. The result will be a shot that starts to the left of target but slices to the right more viciously than before.

Bearing this procedure in mind, let's consider the specific faulty flights of the ball.

Slice (Type 1). Ball starts to the left of the target line, then curves to the right.

This is the most common type of slice—a real "slicer's slice," if you like. Since the ball starts left, the swing path through impact is obviously from outside to in, and the clubface position at impact is open to the swing path.

The first thing to correct is the open clubface position at impact that causes the curve to the right. To do this, you should:

1. Check clubface is not set open to the swing path in the setup. (This by itself could cause the slice.)

2. Check your hold is not what is technically called too "weak," which means that either the left hand or both hands are turned too far to the left. Even if the club were set square to the swing path, a "weak" hold would result in the clubface opening at impact.

3. Check you are not opening the clubface during the swing. Use the "swing-and-stop" method (see page 77) to make certain you have not rolled the clubface open going back. Also check for a free arm swing through the ball; trying to "push" the arms through can leave the clubface in an open position at impact.

If you have taken steps 1, 2, and 3, and you still get a curve to the right, you will have to consider turning both hands slightly to the right into what is called a "strong" position. The hold we recommended earlier had the hands in such a position that if you opened them, both palms would be parallel or "square" to the clubface. Nevertheless, if the only way you can hit the ball straight is to adopt a "strong" position of the hands, then do it. It's infinitely preferable to slicing the ball. We can't tell you exactly how far to turn your hands to the right because this will vary from individual to individual, but basically you should move both hands over, as a unit, until the ball goes straight.

Having corrected the slice, you must now correct the "outside-in" swing path.

1. Check your alignment is correct. If you're pulling the ball, nine times out of ten you'll find that this is where your problem lies. Broadly speaking, there are two ways in which you can be misaligned to the left of the target. In the first, your feet, hips, and shoulders are all aligned to the left of the target. This is the easiest to correct, since in essence you have merely been making a straight shot to the left. Pay particular attention when spreading your feet from the "feet together" position that a line across the toes is parallel to the target line.

In this regard, we might remind you of the "two club" alignment aid we discussed earlier. To use it here, set up to the target normally and put a club down across your toe line. Then go behind the ball, looking down toward the target, and place the other club just outside the ball and parallel to the target line. If you're aiming to the left, this will immediately become apparent to you. If you are misaligned to the left, place the "toe-line" club parallel to the "target-line" club and practice your "countdown" pattern of taking the set, paying particular attention to setting up square to the target line. If you have been setting up too far left, the correct alignment will feel awkward at first—but persevere: It will feel comfortable after a while.

More insidious, and more difficult to spot, is the misalignment in which your feet are square to the target line but your shoulders are aligned to the left. This by itself will cause you to pull the ball because the alignment of the shoulders governs to a large extent the direction of the arm swing. If the shoulders are aligned to the left of target, the arms pull across the ball at impact. To check this, take hold of a club with your hands shoulder distance apart and bring the club up to shoulder level so the left hand touches the left shoulder and the right hand the right shoulder. Now see where the club points. If it points to the left of a line parallel to the target line, then there's your problem. When correcting the shoulder position, check to see that a rigid right arm in the set is not the root of the problem. (Reread the section on correct setup that deals with the shoulders and arms.) Also check to see that your ball position is correct; slicers tend to play the ball too far forward—off the left toe instead of off the left heel.

2. Check you have made a full shoulder turn. If you only partially turn your shoulders going back, they will unwind too quickly coming through the ball, pulling arm swing and club to the left of target. A good way to check this is to have a friend position himself behind you, looking down towards the target. If you've made a full shoulder turn, the clubshaft, at the top, should lie in a line parallel to the target line. If it lies on a line pointing to the left of parallel, your shoulder turn was inadequate.

3. Check you have released your whole right side through the ball. If the right side "sticks" on the downswing, your arms will pull across the ball, resulting in an outside-to-inside swing path.

Slice (*Type* 2). Ball starts straight, then curves to the right.

Here the only problem is the curve to the right. Points to check are the same as in correcting the curve to the right under Type 1: square clubface position in the set, correct hold on the club, and square clubface throughout the swing.

Slice (*Type* 3). Ball starts to the right of the target line and curves farther to the right.

Again, the first problem is the curve caused by the open clubface.

Consult the three points discussed under Type 1.

Having corrected the slice, you must next correct the path of the swing, which is obviously too far from inside to out, compared to the correct swing path.

1. Check your alignment is correct. If you're pushing the ball, this is the place to begin. As you did in correcting the pull, use the "two club" alignment aid to determine whether your whole body is aligned to the right of target. If your feet check out, use the "club-across-the-shoulders" drill to see whether the shoulders alone are at fault. Actually, when your shoulders are aligned too far to the right of target, it is what could be called a "good golfer's" fault. For it is caused by an exaggeration of the correct set of the shoulders and arms—in other words, you are so conscious of "left arm straight, left shoulder up, right shoulder down, right arm soft and in to the side" that you force the left shoulder too far to the right. However, it is a destructive fault. With your shoulders aligned to the right, the whole arm swing is misdirected to the right of target. Practice taking the set and checking with the "club-across-the-shoulders" drill until you build up a feel of the correct, square shoulder alignment.

In the same way that pullers tend to play the ball progressively too far forward in the stance, pushers tend to play the ball progressively too far back in the stance. When you've got yourself lined up correctly, check to see that your ball is off the left heel and not back too far toward the right foot.

2. Check you have not "overturned" the shoulders. (Yes, that may sound as though we have taken leave of our senses, since we said you make a full shoulder turn on every full swing.) We're using the term "overturn" the shoulders here in a specialized sense. What typically happens is that the golfer does not set his right leg slightly inwards in the setup. When he swings back, there is no resistance in the inner thigh muscle of the right leg to the coiling of the upper body. As a result, the hips continue to turn past the 45-degree point that is normal until, at the top of the swing, they have turned almost as much as the shoulders. At the top of the body, this means that the shoulders have turned past their normal full windup position, and the clubshaft will not be on a line parallel to the target line, as it should be, but will point rather to the right of target. If you swing down from that position without making any correction, the path of the swing will be aligned to the right and you will push the ball. Again, a friend can help you to determine whether the clubshaft at the top is in correct position.

3. Check whether you have moved your body past the ball at im-

pact. Remember, we said that there should be a specific "order of movement" in the swing. On the downswing the arm swing should lead, and the release of the right side from the bottom up should time the blade into the ball. However, if you attempt to lead too much with the legs, what usually happens is that you slide laterally with the hips and legs, carrying the upper part of the body with them. By impact, the whole body is ahead of the ball, and the arm swing has, so to speak, been left behind. The body being ahead of the arm swing, the arms can only swing out to right field, pushing the ball.

Another way in which it is common to "slide" past the ball is also attributable to lack of "right leg set." If you set up with slack legs, you can fall into the habit of sliding the hips to the right on the backswing (this faulty action carries the upper body to the right as well). On the downswing, you slide the hips and upper body to the left toward the target, and again the body is ahead of the ball at impact, pushing the ball to the right. If you position a friend in front of you and make a few swings, your friend can easily spot this fault for you by the lateral motion back and forth of the head. The correction is basic: Set up properly, paying particular attention to the "leg set," and coil and recoil—don't "slide and slide."

Hook (*Type 1*). Ball starts to the right of the target line, then curves to the left.

Here the correction of the curve to the left involves correcting the closed clubface in relation to the swing path. To do this, you should:

1. Check the clubface is not set closed in relation to the swing path.
2. Check your hold is not too "strong," which means that both hands are turned too far to the right on the grip. A "strong" hold can lead to the hands returning instinctively to the "square" position at impact, thus closing the blade.
3. Check you are not closing the blade somewhere during the swing. Use the "swing-and-stop" method (see page 77) at the halfway point and at the top of the swing to check that you have not manipulated the blade into a closed position.

In the same way that "pushing" the arms slows the arm swing and leaves the blade open at impact, so can too fast an arm swing close the blade at impact. We hear you say, But I'm supposed to have a fast arm swing! True, but a fast arm swing *without a quick enough release from the right side of the downswing* will lead to closing the blade. This is why, when you watch the touring pros driving the long ball, you will see them releasing very quickly with the right side. As we've said, it's the release that times the blade into the ball. So, if you have a fast arm swing, you can't afford a "dead" right leg; you'd be hooking all over the place. The correction is obvious: You must work on setting the right leg correctly to begin with and then coiling the upper body around a firm right leg. Then it will release correctly in the downswing and square the blade up at impact.

In the same way that a "slicer" must, as a last resort, go to a "stronger" hold, so a "hooker" should go to a slightly "weaker" hold if the hook persists. You should "weaken" the hold until the hook disappears.

To correct the "push" part of this type of hook, the overly "inside-to-out" swing path, refer to the correction of the relevant portion of the Type 3 slice.

Hook (Type 2). Ball starts straight, then curves to the left.

Here the only problem is the closed clubface. Refer to the relevant portion of Type 1 hook.

Hook (Type 3). Ball starts to the left of the target line and curves farther to the left.

Again, we have already covered the corrections above. To correct the closed clubface, see Type 1 hook. To correct the outside-in swing path, the "pull" part of the action, see the relevant portion of the Type 1 slice.

For the sake of completeness, we'll point out that you can have a pure "pull" or a pure "push" (i.e., without any curve). To correct the pure "pull," refer to the relevant portion of the Type 1 slice; to correct the pure "push," refer to the discussion of the Type 3 slice.

The Four Fundamentals

In the course of the six preceding chapters, we have explained the importance of a true swinging action, we have taught you how to hold the club and set up to the ball, and you have progressed from the mini-swing with the 7-iron to the full swing with that club and with the others. We have even offered an advanced course in perfecting the swing. We do believe that any intelligent golfer who follows our instruction will develop a fine, free swing.

However, it's been our experience that many golfers need quick help *right now!* They need to grasp the underlying fundamentals of the swing that will enable them to work out of a slump or to find a quick correction when out on the course with their golfing worlds collapsing around their ears.

To overcome this problem we developed the Four Fundamentals.

These have enabled us to help our pupils quickly and to give them something solid to take home with them in addition to the principles of the true swing. The Four Fundamentals in no way replace the true swinging action; they are, in fact, the four major fundamentals of the swing—and at the same time they are the four major areas in which our pupils' swings tend to go off the track. They are an integral part of the Obitz/Farley system.

Without further ado, the Four Fundamentals are:

1. Alignment
2. Shoulder Turn
3. Tilt
4. Release

You know three of them already, but we will comment on each to put them all in perspective.

Alignment. By now you appreciate the importance of square alignment. We pounded in its importance while discussing the setup, and you have just been through the various types of hooks and slices. However, when working with the Alignment fundamental in your own game, we want you to think of Alignment with a capital A. It's not just the alignment of the feet that is important; for a straight shot to result, the clubface must be square, the hold must be square, and not only the feet, but the hips and shoulders, too, must be squarely aligned. As you've seen, if any of these are misaligned, the swing can be ruined.

An interesting point about clubface alignment is that, by having the clubface square in the set, you're more apt to swing the club on the correct plane. However, if you inadvertently set the blade open to start with, you can easily fall into a flat roundhouse swing in which you work the arms and the club around the body and open the blade still more on the backswing. Then, of course, you have to close the blade coming through the ball to try to hit it squarely. The opposite applies if you set the blade closed in the set: You'll tend to close the blade even more going back, and you'll tend to swing the arms up on far too upright a plane. On the downswing you again have to compensate by opening the blade, otherwise you'll never hit the ball squarely. Now can you appreciate the virtue of a square clubface in the set?

Shoulder Turn. The Shoulder Turn is a *full* turn of the shoulders on the backswing in response to the upward swing of the arms.

The first point to be made about the Shoulder Turn is that, unless you turn the shoulders with the arms and turn them fully, you're going to be *lifting* the club with your hands or your arms rather than swinging. If you lift with the hands, you will twist the blade out of a square position, making it difficult to return the blade to the ball squarely and to hit it straight. If you lift with your arms, you're taking the club up too vertically above the plane of the correct swing, and you will probably chop right down into the ground. Without the shoulders responding fully to the arm swing, you can't swing.

The full turn of the shoulders helps to provide proper timing to the swing. If you make a Shoulder Turn, but happen inadvertently to open or close the clubface a little with the hands, the full shoulder turn gives you time to readjust the blade with your hands on the downswing so that you can meet the ball squarely. Without a Shoulder Turn, the action is more rushed, and you don't have the time to make the necessary compensation.

The Shoulder Turn also assures you of the proper weight transference. If you turn the shoulders fully, you know that your weight has shifted with the turn. You're then in position to let your body come into the shot behind the swing to give you all the power you need. If you don't make a full shoulder turn, too much weight is left on the left foot at the top, and you have to force with the arms and hands. When you do that, you're probably going to mishit the ball—or if you do catch it, you won't have a great deal of power.

Tilt. "Tilt" describes the angle the back makes with the ground as you view the golfer from behind, looking down toward the target. We introduced you to Tilt earlier in this book, but only in regard to establishing the correct tilt at address. Now we want to tell you the whole story, which is vital to the proper understanding of the last section of this chapter, in which we deal with topped, thin, and fat shots.

One of the most common faults that we find in the pupils who come to our schools is that they fail to establish the correct tilt in the set. We see several main types of incorrect tilt.

The first occurs in the golfers who have been told that they should stand straight up to the ball. These golfers don't tilt forward from the waist at all, and their whole body is set too vertically; this in turn causes a rigid set to the arms as the golfer reaches down for the ball from too great a height. The main problem with this "vertical" tilt is that, because the shoulders rotate at right angles to the spine, the swing plane that it establishes is nearly horizontal to the ground—far too flat, in golfer's parlance. This swing plane would be fine for a baseball swing, where the ball comes at you in the air, but it obviously won't do for the golf ball that lies on the ground in front of you.

The second type of incorrect tilt we see occurs in the golfer who has been told to bend his knees. These people also acquire too vertical a tilt to the back. They think they are making the correct tilt by bending their knees, but in fact they don't tilt forward at all; they just squat down with an excessive bend of the knees, leaving their back vertical. Again, this sets up too flat a swing plane.

The third type of tilt problem appears in the golfer who slouches over the ball. This guy bends forward much too far from the waist, letting his shoulders and head drop forward. Generally, such a player is very rigid in the knees; he's stiff-legged because he has forced the weight of his upper body out over his toes. To counterbalance himself, he is forced to push back his knees and his seat. No golfer can swing from such a locked position. Equally bad, he's bent so far forward that the swing plane he establishes is far too upright to be practical for golf.

The first two golfers, who stood with too vertical a tilt, are going to realize subconsciously, at some point during the swing, that they are swinging on too horizontal a plane. They will then compensate by tilting forward more. In the same way, the third golfer, who tilted forward excessively, will compensate by raising the tilt of the body. But making such moves during the swing—by so doing, you are in effect changing both the axis and the plane of the swing—makes it extremely difficult to catch the ball flush. The reason? It's almost impossible to make an exact compensating move.

This leads to the second important factor about Tilt: You must not only establish the correct tilt in the set, *you must maintain that same angle between the back and the ground throughout the swing.*

If you maintain the correct tilt throughout the swing, you will get the proper shoulder turn and your arms will swing the club up on a perfect plane. Maintain the Tilt properly and you'll rotate the shoulders around the spine correctly. However, don't confuse the two; that rotation around the spine is the *result* of maintaining the Tilt. Never try to rotate your shoulders around the spine—it won't guarantee that you're going to keep the Tilt, and trying to turn around the spine will freeze the average golfer (it kills his freedom of movement). The thought of maintaining the Tilt will allow the golfer to swing the arms and turn the shoulders freely.

If you don't maintain the Tilt, then no sort of consistency of swing can result. This is because the body works up and down, raising and lowering the clubhead as it does so.

Release. Throughout this book, we've emphasized the importance of the right side releasing in the downswing. You release from the bottom up, from the right heel to the right knee to the right hip—and this keeps the uncoiling of the shoulders until last. Then, between the

A

B

C

The correct "Tilt"—the angle the back makes with the ground when you view the golfer from behind looking down toward the target—is one of the most important fundamentals of the swing. To strike the ball accurately, you must not only establish the correct "Tilt" in the set (A), but maintain the "Tilt" throughout the swing (B and C).

uncoiling of the shoulders and the arm swing, you can time the blade into the ball. By releasing the right side you are able to accelerate through the ball; releasing the right side gives you full extension through the ball and gets the weight flowing correctly into the shot.

The one point we have learned in teaching the Release is not to be dogmatic about how you feel it. Everyone will feel the swing a little differently, and the same is true of the Release. Some 50 percent of our pupils find that the thought of letting the right heel rise induces the proper release of the right side, 30 percent feel it as a releasing of the right knee, and 10 percent feel that the hips make the initial move of the lower body in the downswing. The other 10 percent may feel everything from a push of the right foot to a release of the whole right side! So we say use whichever "feel" strikes your fancy. Don't tie yourself up in knots trying for a "feel" which doesn't work for you. The one "must" of the Release is that the right knee must finish pointing forward of the original ball position.

Now that you have absorbed the Four Fundamentals, we would like to return to our consideration of how the ball reacts. We deliberately left two types of flight until last—the high ball and the low ball and the faulty flights related to them: topped shots, skied shots, and so on. You will appreciate our having explained the Four Fundamentals beforehand.

High Balls, Low Balls, Topped Balls, "Fat" Balls

In studying the trajectory a ball will take—normal, high, or low—it is essential to understand one fact at the very start: A ball goes high or low depending on where you hit it. If you hit the ball on the top half, it's going to fly low. If you hit it on the bottom half, it's going to fly high. It's that simple.

Let's take this a step further. Basically, too steep an angle of descent into the ball will drive the ball low because you're contacting the ball above center. And too shallow an angle of descent will drive the ball high because you're contacting the ball below center.

When individual golfers need to correct faulty height of trajectory, there are always many possible reasons for the problem in each case. Here we find it helpful to divide golfers into two broad categories:

1. The golfer who is striking the ball reasonably well. The only real problem is that the trajectory of the ball is too high or too low.

2. The golfer who is not only getting shots that are too high or too low, but is afflicted as well by such bad mishits as topped balls, "fat" shots, slices, and pulls.

In dealing first with the better golfer, we would specify three main areas to check for both the ball hit too low and the ball hit too high.

Ball Hit Too Low

Ball Too Far Back in the Stance. If you play the ball too far back toward the right foot, you will contact the ball when the clubhead is still descending rather than catch the ball when the clubhead is at the bottom of the arc. This has two effects: You reduce the effective loft of the club and you hit a little more on the top of the ball than usual. So the ball flies lower than normal.

Weight Too Far Forward in the Set. You should set up with the weight equally divided between the feet. If you set up with too much weight on the left foot and keep it there during the swing, you will reduce the effective loft on the club and steepen the arc into the ball.

Weight Shifted Too Quickly in the Downswing. If the legs make their move too early in the downswing, and too much weight is transferred to the left foot too soon, this will steepen the arc of the downswing. Again, you will contact the ball at a higher point than normal, driving the ball low.

Ball Hit Too High

Ball Too Far Forward in the Stance. When you play the ball forward of the normal position about opposite the left heel, you will contact the ball after the lowest point in the downswing arc. The clubhead is then ascending. This has two effects: You increase the effective loft of the club and you hit a little more on the bottom half of the ball. So the ball flies higher than normal.

Weight Too Far Back in the Set. If you set up with more weight on the right foot than on the left, and keep it there during the swing, you will increase the effective loft on the club and contact the ball more on the bottom half.

Weight Held Back in the Downswing. If the right side does not release properly in the downswing, too much weight is left on the right foot through the hitting area. This has the effect of making the downswing arc too shallow. You contact the ball below the equator, driving the ball up. (An extreme case of this could lead to "fat" shots.)

When you come to the poorer golfer, you find more points to check, but they are all, as you will see, basic points. The problem, essentially, is that the golfer involved has not learned the true swing.

Ball Hit Thin, Too Low, or Topped

The Tilt. The fundamental most commonly violated with this type of mishit is the Tilt. Either the golfer adopts an incorrect tilt in the set or alters his tilt during the swing. If he sets up with too vertical a tilt and fails to compensate during the swing, he can hit the ball thin, too low, or top it, depending on the severity of the faulty posture adopted. This type of mishit can also be caused by bending forward too much in reaching for the ball or slouching too far over the ball. What can happen then is that the golfer reacts by raising his tilt during the swing.

If the golfer raises his tilt during the swing, and makes no compensation, this type of mishit can occur. However, it could happen that the golfer lowers his tilt during the backswing and reacts by raising it in the downswing. This, too, can cause thin, low, or topped balls. If you're raising your tilt going back, you're "lifting" with the arms or shoulders rather than swinging. And if you're lowering the tilt going back, watch out for increased bending of the knees in the backswing. This is quite common, as it gives a false illusion of power.

Outside-in Swing Path. If you're swinging outside-to-in through the ball, this steepens the arc of the swing and in turn results in contacting the ball not only on the outside edge (golfer's point of view) but also more on the top side. This will tend to drive the ball low. If you're a golfer who tends to combine pulls with pull-slices and outright topped balls, this is the action you have to correct. (As we've told you, the correct path of the swing is from inside-to-square-to-inside. The correct swing path results in the club contacting the ball when it is traveling parallel to the ground.)

Slide-and-slide Swing. We met this type of fault earlier in the chapter; the point we'll make here is that it can also cause you to hit the ball thin or even to top it. If you sway to the right, obviously you move the arc of the swing to the right, too. If you don't compensate exactly in the downswing, a mishit will result. If you don't sway forward enough, the low point of the arc will be behind the ball, and you can catch the top half of the ball, thinning or topping it—or merely sending it low, if you're lucky. If you sway forward too far, you can catch the top part of the ball, driving it low or even smothering it. This is the most unpredictable type of swing because it can cause "fat" shots and shots hit too high as well. Leave swaying to the trees—it's death to a swing!

The Reverse Weight Shift. When you set up with far too much weight on the left foot in a full swing, what usually happens is that you not only keep the weight on the left foot in the backswing, but you bend the left knee more, leaving all the weight on the left foot at the top of the swing. In the downswing you react by shifting the weight to the right foot. As you know, this is exactly the opposite of the correct shift of weight that should take place—hence the name, "reverse weight shift."

When you have all the weight on the right foot as you come through the ball, it moves the arc of the swing to the right, or behind the ball. Sometimes the club will hit the ground in back of the ball, bounce up, and strike the top half of the ball, topping or at least hitting it thin. Sometimes you're lucky and "drop kick" the blade into the back of the ball. The ball will then fly quite well, but you will have lost power. More often, you hit in back of the ball and hit it "fat." The point is that if you're hitting mostly "fat" and occasionally thin or top the ball, the "reverse weight shift" can be the cause.

Ball Hit Too High or "Fat"

The Tilt. The fundamentals most commonly violated are the Tilt and the Release.

As regards the Tilt, an incorrect tilt at address or altering the tilt during the swing can be the cause. If you set up with too vertical a tilt and then compensate by lowering the tilt during the swing, you can get underneath the ball too much, skying it or—more extreme—hitting it "fat." If you bend forward too much or reach for the ball, you put your weight on your toes, and on the downswing the weight often can be thrown farther forward—and you sky the ball or hit it "fat."

If you raise the tilt during the swing, you will often become aware of this subconsciously and try to compensate by lowering the tilt in the downswing. If you overdo the compensation, you will sky or hit "fat." If you lower the tilt during the backswing and make no compensation, you can again sky the ball or hit it "fat."

As regards the Release, failure to release the right side in the downswing will force the hands to take over and "flick" the clubhead, resulting in hitting the ball fat or skying it.

Inside-out Swing Path. In the same way that too outside-to-in a swing path makes the downswing arc too steep, too inside-to-out a swing path makes the path of the swing too shallow as it goes through the ball. If you're a golfer who tends to combine pushes with push-hooks and occasional high or "fat" balls of the push or push-hook variety, you need to correct this faulty swing path before you do anything else. Swinging your forearms a bit more vertically (up and down) is your best correction.

Slide-and-slide Swing. This faulty swing can cause high or "fat" shots as the result of where you contact the ball. If you compensate only partly for the sway, you can strike the ground behind the ball, hitting it "fat"; if you're a little farther forward, you can catch the lower part of the ball, driving it high. The message is that if you combine thin, topped, "fat," and high balls, the slide-and-slide swing is a good point to check. To stop the slide, turn your shoulders around the upper spine a little sooner.

The Reverse Weight Shift. See the discussion of this topic in the previous section on thin, low, and topped balls. Also not dropping the left shoulder as it turns will help shift the weight smoothly and correctly.

We'll conclude this chapter with an observation and a suggestion. One of the biggest reasons why golfers don't progress as they should is that they don't understand why the ball flies straight, crooked, high, or low. How many times have you heard the cry You looked up! to a golfer who has just topped the ball? There's one of the major misconceptions in golf today. You can't really "look up"; the head cannot pull the body away from the ball. (That would be like the tail wagging the dog.) *Incorrect body action is what moves the head*, not the other way around. This is true whether the head moves up, down, or sideways.

We would like to suggest—no, *we'll insist*—that from this day on you keep a notebook on your own game. Into this notebook should go key thoughts you find useful in maintaining a free swing and—very important—a list of the faults that you tend to make. You will outgrow some faults, but many faults you may never totally overcome. Which particular faults will recur with you? That's anyone's guess, because every golfer is individual. A notebook will provide you with a checklist of regularly recurring faults to consult when your game is off.

Many golfers never really learn the game; they're forever running to the pro for a correction that they should have learned for themselves. Your objective should be to grow in knowledge as a golfer so that when your game goes off you can at least work intelligently *with* your professional rather than wait helplessly for the magic word.

OBITZ AND FARLEY SAY:

1. Whether the ball flies straight or crooked is determined by: first, the path of the swing and, second, the clubface alignment in relation to that path at impact.

2. To cure a misdirected curve ball, you must first correct the curve, then correct the "push" or "pull" part of the problem. Attempting the reverse procedure is one of the main reasons why "curve ball hitters" remain "curve ball hitters."

3. In the Obitz/Farley golf system, quick help for the ailing golf swing is supplied by the Four Fundamentals: Alignment, Shoulder Turn, The Tilt, and The Release.

4. What makes a ball fly high or low is where you hit it. If you hit the bottom half of the ball, it's going to fly high; if you hit the top half, it's going to fly low.

5. The basic reasons for hitting the ball too high or too low, topping it, or hitting it "fat" are: incorrect ball position, faulty weight distribution in the set, faulty motions during the swing that lead to incorrect weight shift, moving the whole swing arc to the right or left, raising or lowering the Tilt, and making the descent of the clubhead into the ball too steep or too shallow.

8
Different Swings Make
Different Shots

WHEN YOU MENTION SHOTMAKING to most people, they think in terms
of deliberately hooking and slicing the ball or hitting it high or low.
Those things are part of shotmaking, but the words "shotmaking" and
"shotmaker" mean a good deal more than that.

The winners, those golfers who not only win tournaments but
whose game will stand up to the pressure of winning major titles, have
the swing and the rhythm and the tempo which are the result of perfect
coordination of the arm swing with the body coil. They can take a little
off the ball or put a little more on it, where the run-of-the-mill tour
player cannot.

All the great swingers have been great shotmakers. You don't have
to go back to such people as Bobby Jones and Tommy Armour, both
fine swingers and fine shotmakers, or even to Ben Hogan, who could
make any kind of a shot—low with a fade, high with a draw, you name
it! Sam Snead is a great shotmaker, Julius Boros is a great shotmaker,
Gene Littler is a great shotmaker, and Don January is a great shotmaker.
And who has more shots in his bag than Jack Nicklaus, Johnny Miller,
Billy Casper, Tom Kite, Ray Floyd, Ben Crenshaw or Jerry Pate? They
all have the ability to create the shot for the occasion, whereas the golfer
in the pack, who comes close but doesn't win, just doesn't have a swing
good enough to produce the necessary shots.

If the great swingers are the great shotmakers, the inference should be obvious: You have to learn the swing, the true swinging action, before you can ever be a shotmaker. You have to learn to swing with a good, even tempo before you can learn to vary it. And you have to learn to hit the ball reasonably straight and with good trajectory before you can learn to curve the ball deliberately or vary the trajectory.

Much of what we will cover in this chapter is advanced golf. You have to be prepared to put in a lot of time on the practice ground in order to master the more difficult shots. But it will be time well spent, for at the end of the trail is your goal: becoming a complete golfer.

We'd like to modify that last thought a little—for the phrase "complete golfer," let us substitute "complete swinger." You will find as you progress that you are not so much learning "shots" as you are learning slightly different *swings* that will create the shots for you. There is a difference, and it is an important one. To vary the normal swing, you in fact land up with an armory of different swings to meet every occasion. If you always think "swing," you will never go far wrong.

Varying Swing Tempo

Most golfers are far more interested in learning the technique of, say, bending the ball to the right or left than they are in learning to vary the tempo of the swing. That's a pity; varying the tempo is a basic skill, one that you will use every time you're out on the golf course; bending a ball around an obstacle is something you will use only occasionally.

The first point we want to make about the swing tempo is that you never swing with your maximum speed. You'll remember that we told you early in the book that the first thing you must learn is to use only about 80 percent of maximum as your highest speed of swing (or your normal speed of swing, if you prefer). Anything greater than 80 percent will run you the risk of levering, or heaving with the large muscles of the body, and losing the swing.

However, it is apparent that you can use a faster swing off the tee when you have a big target—say, a 50-yard-wide landing area—than when you have to put the ball on a smaller target, such as a green. And you must be even more careful if you have to land the ball on a 15-square-foot area or you're out of business. Golf courses are set up so that the shorter the approach shot you have, the more hazards you will usually encounter. This in turn means you have to be able to control the tempo of your swing in order to get the precision you need. It can make sense, for example, to play an easy 7-iron rather than a hard 8-iron where the target is small.

Another consideration in playing to a green is whether you want the ball to land with plenty of backspin or with less backspin. This is a product of the speed of swing you use. A slower swing than normal will reduce the amount of backspin you put on the ball. Your normal swing tempo which is slightly faster, will put more backspin on the ball.

When you want to vary the tempo of the swing, you have to get back to the basics of swinging. As we've said before, the arms make the swing and the body times the blade into the ball. So when you want to establish a particular tempo on a certain swing, you have to ask yourself, How fast do I want to swing my arms? Once you've established the tempo of the arm swing, the body will respond with the appropriate amount of action to time the swing.

If you want to hit the ball gently, just let the weight of the arms and the club work in the downswing. Simply let them drop and swing through—and you will get a very soft shot. If you swing the arms a little quicker, you'll get a slightly firmer shot.

The best way to practice varying the tempo of the swing is to take one club—preferably the 7-iron in this case—and try to hit the ball different distances with the same length of swing. To do that, of course, you have to vary the tempo.

Harry Obitz tells of watching Jack Nicklaus practice.

Harry Obitz: Nicklaus takes a short iron and he plays gentle little shots that only go chip-shot distances, but the amazing thing is that in sending the ball this short distance, he is swinging the club back past the halfway point in the backswing. He moves the club so slowly you can almost read the label on the club as it swings through the ball! Then, by moving the club a little bit farther back and a little more quickly, he makes the ball take on added distance. And he can do the same sort of thing with the full swing. He makes a full arm swing and body coil but swings at such a slow tempo that the ball only goes half the normal distance; then he increases the tempo and force in the swing until he gets full distance with the club.

We think so much of this type of practice that we have Dave Marr demonstrate it at our schools. Dave, of course, is a superb swinger of the club, and it always amazes our pupils to see how he can hit the ball 30 yards with a full 7-iron swing, then 50 yards, 75 yards, 100 yards, and up to about 130 yards.

Now your reaction to all this may well be, Nicklaus can do it and Dave Marr can do it, but isn't that too difficult for me? Yes, it's difficult. And we speak from first-hand experience because we have practiced this way ourselves for years. But get out there and *start* on it! If you become only half as skillful at it as we are, or as Marr or Nicklaus are, you'll still be miles ahead of the majority of golfers. And we're speaking not only of amateurs, but professionals as well. We all know the amateur who prides himself on hitting a 160-yard, par 3 hole with a 7-iron! But it's the same with the pros. There are guys out on the tour who think only of hitting the ball hard and square. So they're out there seven or eight years, they've never won, and their game always falls apart on the rare occasion that they're in contention. They're always asking themselves, What more do I have to do? They've never learned to vary the tempo of the swing!

When you really become good at varying the tempo of the swing, you can take care of the guys who hawk your bag on a par-3 to see what club you took. You simply take a "soft" swing with a far stronger club than most people would use on the hole—and watch your opponent blink! Sam Snead is a master at this. He will take a 6-iron and hit the ball 130 yards and make sure his "bag-hawking" opponent knows it! Julius Boros can do the same. But perhaps the greatest of them all was Dutch Harrison. Harry Obitz remembers how Dutch used to handle it.

Harry Obitz: Back in the old hustling days, Dutch liked to take young guys just coming onto the tour out for a game. He'd say, "Come on, let's play a few holes." And the next thing he'd say would be, "Well, we may as well play for the caddie fee." All he wanted was the $5 for the caddie.

So they would come to a par-3 hole, and it's 160 yards long, and Dutch looks at the hole and says, "Jeez, that looks like a 3-iron." He takes the 3-iron and puts a little soft swing on it and cosies the ball up 10 feet from the hole. Now the young guy doesn't know what to do. He either swings full and barrels right over the green or he holds back on the shot and sends it into the lake. Whatever happened, Dutch had shot your whole swing down—and he had your $5!

How to Hook and Slice

If you had just read the last chapter and understood the principles that govern why a ball in flight will curve to the left or right, and if you asked yourself, How can I do those things deliberately?, you would probably answer in this fashion: That's easy! To hook the ball, all I have to do is align myself to the right of the target so that my swing path is to the right of target, and then set the blade square to the target so that it is closed in relation to the swing path. To slice the ball, I'd just set up left of the target so the swing path is to the left of target, and then set the blade square to the target so that it is open in relation to that swing

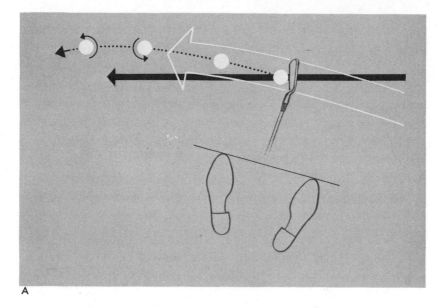

A

A simple way to hook the ball deliberately is to set up to the right of target, but set the blade square to the target, so that it is closed in relation to the swing path (A). To slice, reverse the procedure—set up to the left of target, but set the blade square to the target, so that it is open in relation to the swing path (B).

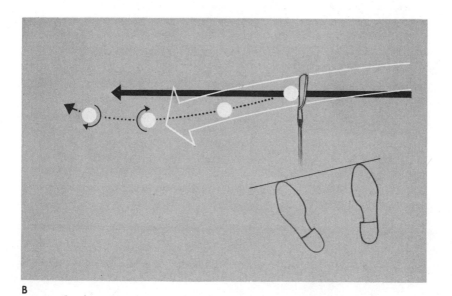

B

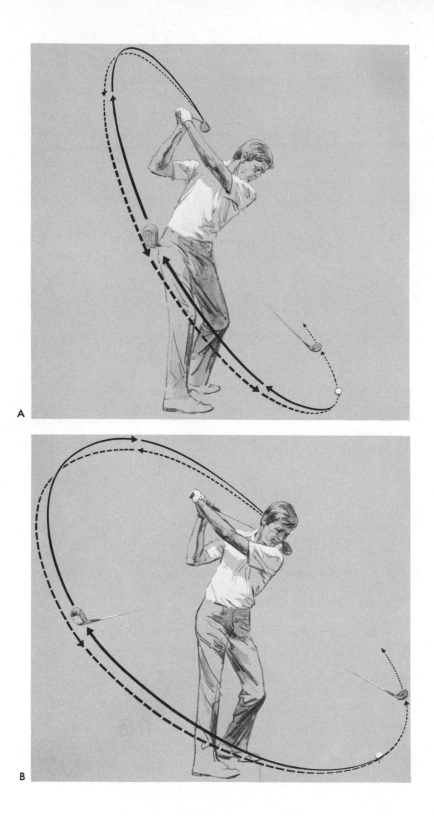

A

B

C

To hook or slice the ball with the swing, you alter the swing plane from the plane you use normally (A). Varying the swing plane induces forearm rotation during the swing, closing or opening the blade as desired at impact. To hook the ball (B), align to the right of the ultimate target, and swing flatter than normal. Swinging back, the forearms will rotate the blade into a slightly open position; swinging through the ball, the forearms will react and close the blade, putting hook-spin on the ball. To slice the ball (C), you set up to the left of the ultimate target, and swing more upright than usual. This will work the blade from closed on the backswing, to open coming through the ball, putting slice-spin on the ball.

path. Once I make these adjustments, I can just swing away normally and the ball will hook or slice.

All this is very true. The ball will hook or slice, and this is a valid way to do it. It is also a good place for the less experienced player to experiment with deliberate hooks and slices. However, this is not the only way to do it; you can also work the ball with the swing.

To hook the ball with the swing, set up with your alignment to the right of your ultimate target (the point you want the ball to curve back to) but don't change anything else in the set. When you swing back, swing back with the thought that you are going to swing on a slightly flatter plane than normal. When you swing back flatter than normal, your forearms will tend to rotate the club into a slightly open position. Now, as you come through the ball, the forearms will react, closing the blade and putting hook-spin on the ball. In other words, in the backswing you allow your left forearm to roll over your right, and on the downswing you allow the right forearm to roll over the left. The point is that you achieve this forearm rotation simply by swinging a little flatter than normal and allowing the rotation to take place. In this way you are still swinging; you don't have to put sudden moves on the clubhead, moves which you would invariably try to make with the hands, thereby ruining the shot.

To slice the ball, do exactly the opposite. Set up to the left of the ultimate target and swing back on a more upright plane than usual. When you do this, the forearms will react by closing the blade slightly on the backswing. Coming through the ball, they will react the other way and open the blade, putting the desired slice-spin on the ball.

In changing the plane of the swing, the key to putting the club in the right plane is the cocking action of the right arm—the windup action of the right arm in the backswing that we discussed earlier. You do it this way: Suppose you normally swing back to a point over your right shoulder at the top of the swing. To swing back more upright than usual, think of swinging the arms back to a point closer to your neck. To swing back flatter, swing back to a point outside your right shoulder. But the action that permits you to do that is the cocking of the right arm. If you want a more upright swing than usual, you have to let the right arm go farther from the right side at the top of the swing (in the same way that Jack Nicklaus does). And if you want a flatter swing, you have to allow the right elbow to stay closer to the right side than usual.

When we talk about making a more upright swing or a flatter swing in order to produce hooks and slices, we are not speaking of radical changes from your normal swing plane, but *very subtle changes*. For a fade you might swing up with the feel of, say, half an inch closer to the right ear than normal—and perhaps one inch for a slice. The measures would be similar for a draw and a hook. However, because the changes in the swing plane are subtle, you can vary it infinitely; you will be able to feel yourself putting a slightly different swing on the ball.

Here we would like to cite a problem that can occur with the "close or open the blade in the set" school of thought. Remember, if you set the blade in a closed position in the setup, you tend to swing more upright, and if you set it open, you tend to swing flatter. Now, if you apply this to deliberate hooks and slices, what happens? You want to hook the ball, so you set the blade closed. As a result, you could react with a more upright swing. The upright swing, as we've learned, will tend to make you work the blade from closed to open. This can square the blade up again, and instead of the hook you planned for, you may get only a slight draw. The shot you planned will not come off!

The same thing could happen if you try to slice the ball by setting the blade open in the setup. You could react with a flatter swing than normal, work the blade from open to closed, and that slice could turn into a little fade or even a straight shot to the left of target. We should point out, however, that this problem would be most likely to occur with a full swing at your normal tempo, due to the amount of force in the swing. It would not happen, as a rule, with a "softer" swing or with partial swings.

There's one pitfall we'd like to warn you about while you're learning to curve the ball with the swing: Don't attempt to open or close the blade with the hands and wrists. Remember, the forearms swing the club—the hands and wrists do nothing, they just go along for the ride. If your forearms are working the blade from open to closed or from closed to open, you're not going to be trying to close or open the blade with the hands and wrists. If you do use your hands and wrists to manipulate the blade, you will destroy the swinging action.

This raises a point. In order for you to learn how to hook a ball, to slice it, or to hit it straight, you have to know what the forearms are doing. You have to be able to feel whether the forearms are working the blade from open to closed (hook) or from closed to open (slice), or if there is no rotation of the forearms either way (straight ball). This is where the hands come into the picture.

You may remember our saying that the only role of the hands in the golf swing was to feel the club. Now we will amplify that a little. When you want to feel what the clubface is doing during the swing (closing, opening, or remaining square), you have to try to feel what the toe of the club is doing. In the backswing, if the toe is moving faster than the heel of the club, you are opening the blade; if the toe is moving slower than the heel, you are closing the blade. In the downswing, if the toe of the club is moving faster than the heel, you are closing the blade; and if the toe is moving slower than the heel, you are opening the blade. If you are hitting the ball straight, you won't feel any opening or closing action at all. These things you have to learn in practice so that the feel for what the blade is doing—and this feel is found in your fingers—becomes part of your repertoire.

Trying to work the ball with the hands and wrists is a fault that is not confined to amateurs. There are many pros out on the tour who never learn the true swing and as a result never learn to work the ball with the swing. We can think of several who have been on the tour for six or seven years and who thunder the ball—hit the ball hard and square and little else—and putt like demons and still don't win. Their problem is that four or five times during a tournament they get into a position where only a real "shot" will do the job—and to make the shot you have to be a swinger. They try to make the shot by manipulating the club with their hands, and of course the shot doesn't come off. That's how they lose the vital strokes that put them back to fourth or fifth place in the tournament. Then they lose confidence, and soon they're settling for a tenth-place finish. They win money, but they're not champions because they're not swingers and they're not shotmakers.

Hitting the Ball High and Low

Our approach to hitting the ball high or low is the same as that for deliberate hooks and slices. Yes, you can play the ball a little forward in your stance to hit a ball high and back in your stance to hit a low ball. When you play the ball forward, you increase the effective loft on the

When you play the ball back in your stance (A), you decrease the effective loft on the club, resulting in a lower shot than normal (B). When you play the ball forward in our stance (C), you increase the effective loft and get a higher shot than normal.

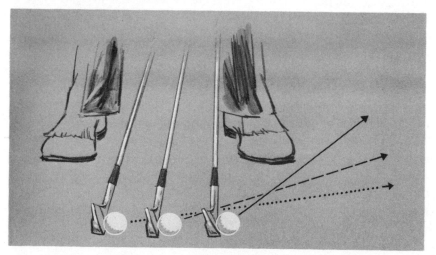

club; when you play it back, you decrease the effective loft by hooding the club slightly. And yes, putting a little more weight on the left foot in the setup will help you hit the ball low, and more weight than normal on the right foot in the set will help you hit the ball high.

But there is another way to do these things: Work the ball with the swing.

The way you work the ball high or low with the swing ties in with our principle that the arms make the swing and the body times the swing. You don't try to flick the ball up high with the hands, nor do you beat down on it. You do it with the body.

You don't make any changes in your setup to the ball or in the backswing. It's the downswing that does the job. If you want to hit the ball low, you shift your weight a little more quickly than usual to your left side. You allow the right side to release a little earlier, which means the arms swing down a little later and you catch the ball a little later, when the blade is a little more hooded, and you drive the ball low.

The reverse applies to hitting the ball high. Here you start the arms swinging down, but you don't let the right side release until a little later than usual. You keep behind the shot a little longer, keep a little more weight than normal on the right side through the hitting area, and you hold the body back a fraction to let the arms and the club pass in front of you sooner, before the body can close the blade. This causes the club to swing upwards sooner, sending the ball higher than usual.

One thought we would like to add on both hooking and slicing the ball and hitting it high and low is this. Whether you decide to make your adjustments in the set or to make the shot with a special type of swing—work it with the swing, as we described it—it is important that you don't get so hung up on the changes you're making that you forget to swing the club. There's a great tendency to introduce leverage of some kind when you're trying to work the ball. The moral is obvious: You must practice these shots before you can use them. You must have total confidence in your ability to make them out on the course. As Ben Hogan once put it so nicely, Never play a shot you haven't practiced recently!

There are many, many ways to make the ball curve or to fly high or low. Here we have only been able to scratch the surface. However, we will say this: You can make your adjustments in the set, you can work the ball with the swing, or you can *combine* the two if you wish. As we said a couple of times earlier, one shouldn't be too dogmatic about golf. Certainly in shotmaking there is more than one road home, and what suits you is what is right for you.

To hit the ball high or low with the swing, you merely release the right side later or earlier. For the high ball (A), release the right side a little later than normal. You stay behind the shot a little longer, which means the club will swing upwards sooner, resulting in the desired high trajectory. For the low ball (B), release the right side a little earlier than normal; the arms swing down later and you catch the ball with the blade a little hooded, driving the ball low.

We should also touch on club selection in regard to these various shots. You should take a stronger or weaker club according to the following observations: By and large if you're hooking the ball, you will get more distance than normal out of a club unless you're hooking the ball so much that it flies low to the ground. If you're fading or slicing the ball, then you're going to lose distance (how much distance depends on how much sidespin you put on the ball). When you're hitting high shots and low shots again you must realize that this will affect distance. If you're going to hit a shot low and have a lot of weight on your left foot at impact, you don't have the advantage of your weight being behind the shot (as in a normal swing), so you're going to lose distance. And if you're hitting the ball high, some of the force you generate will be expended by hitting the ball high—and again you will get less distance than normal.

Playing Trouble Shots

Every golfer, even champion golfers, gets into trouble. How well you get out of trouble depends on how accurately you assess the lie and on intelligent club selection.

Many golfers panic when they get into the rough; worse, they lose their temper and attempt impossible shots. The first rule of coping with rough is to accept the penalty of less distance and then see what is possible in the circumstances.

If you're lying well, the shot can be played normally. Club selection enters the picture when it is impossible for you to apply the clubface to the ball cleanly. If you know that some grass will come between the clubface and the ball at impact, you know that this will reduce backspin and the ball will come out of the rough somewhat lower and will run more. Thus you should select a slightly weaker club than normal in these circumstances.

The deeper the ball lies in the rough, the more likely it is that the grass will twist the blade out of alignment as you swing through the ball. In such circumstances, you must firm up your hold on the club. When you firm up your hold, put more body in the shot—more shoulder action—and release from the right side. This compensates to some degree for the reduced "flailing" action in the wrists resulting from the firmer hold. Really drive that right side through the ball when you're in deep—you'll be surprised how much distance you can get even from a poor lie.

If the ball is deep down in lush grass, and you want to avoid having to cut through a foot of grass before hitting the ball, you may find it necessary to set up with a little more weight on the left foot than usual and to break the wrists a little quicker in the backswing. These adjustments enable you to swing down more cleanly on the ball. However, don't make the mistake in such circumstances of lifting with the arms and shoulders and heaving at the ball. Even though you are cocking the wrists a little quicker, you should still emphasize swinging the arms and permitting the shoulders to respond fully to the arm swing. This action will keep the club in front of you at all times despite the quicker wrist break.

Uphill, Downhill, and Sidehill Lies

These lies are the nemesis of the average golfer. Too often his attitude is one of resentment that he has gotten an uneven lie. Think of these lies instead as a *challenge* to you as a shotmaker. This will keep your mind where it should be—on the steps necessary for making a good swing from these lies.

Uphill and Downhill Lies. There are two schools of thought on these lies. One school says that you should try to make your body as perpendicular to the slope as possible. The idea is that you set yourself up to swing parallel to the slope right at the address. However, on anything other than a very *slight* uphill or downhill lie, this is a very awkward way to stand to the ball. You feel that you must stand there locked in place—and the tendency is to lose the swing.

We favor bending the uphill knee on these lies in order that the body can be more vertical. When you're standing vertically at address, you're in a more normal and natural position, and you can swing back more freely.

On the downhill slope, remember that you have to break the wrists a little more quickly than normal in the backswing. If you don't, you run the risk of the club "sticking" in the hill as you swing back. Don't make the mistake of sitting back on your right leg at the top and trying to "scoop" the ball up; you will only cold-top the ball. Instead, release strongly down the slope, making a special effort to swing the club parallel to the slope. Don't worry if the severity of the slope means you lose your balance in the finish and you have to take a step forward with your right foot to avoid falling over. It's more important to strike the ball cleanly than to have a pretty finish!

Because of the downslope, you effectively reduce the loft of the club you play with. So take a club lofted enough to get the ball up in the air. You'll also find that, because you have to release strongly down the slope in order to contact the ball flush, there's a tendency for the body to get ahead of the ball at impact. This can leave the blade open through the hit, so allow for a push/slice action when setting up to the ball.

On the uphill slope, it's important to kick the right knee in a little more than usual when setting up. There's a tendency from these lies to sway to the right (down the hill) when swinging the club away from the ball. You have to make an extra effort to coil the body in place around the right leg from this lie so that you keep your swing center steady; the slight extra inward set of the right knee helps you accomplish this. As you swing through the ball, the important point again is to swing the club through parallel to the slope. However, this will inevitably leave more weight than normal on the right leg through the hit. This in turn means that it is very easy to pull/hook the ball. (You should align yourself in the set a little to the right of the target to allow for this.)

Again, club selection is a factor. Because you are hitting up the slope, you effectively increase the loft on the club, and you expend more force in hitting the ball up rather than along. For this reason, take a stronger club than you normally would for the distance.

Sidehill Lies. The chief problem with sidehill lies is retaining one's balance: There's a tendency to fall down the slope during the swing because the force generated in the swing will tend to pull you back on your heels when the ball lies above your feet and forward on your toes when the ball lies below your feet. To counteract this tendency, it's important to put your weight more forward on the balls of your feet when the ball is above you and back on your heels when the ball is below you.

When the ball lies above your feet, you have to set up more erectly to the ball than usual and farther away from it. This has the effect of flattening the swing plane so that the ball will curve to the left in a hooking flight pattern. So the first thing to do is to aim to the right of the target to compensate for this right-to-left flight. However, there is a way of setting up in a slightly more normal position—by choking down on the grip of the club (one inch or so on a moderate slope, more if the slope is severe). This has the effect of enabling you to tilt forward a little more from the waist in the normal fashion. To compensate for the loss of distance you get from choking down (choking down narrows the radius of the swing), you should select a slightly stronger club than usual.

Another consideration in selecting a stronger club is that it's most important not to swing too hard when the ball lies above you. As we said, there's a tendency to fall down the hill, so to speak, during the swing. So a smooth, steady swing with a stronger club will be more helpful than a harder swing with a weaker club.

When the ball is below your feet, you have to bend forward more from the waist and reach downward for the ball. This is an unnatural position, but again you can help yourself achieve a more natural position by adjusting your setup. What you should do is select a stronger club than normal for the distance; its extra length will enable you to stand slightly more erect. You should also hold the club as close to the end of the grip as possible without letting the butt of the left hand slip off the grip. The second adjustment is to play the ball closer to your feet.

Whatever you do to make the setup more comfortable, you will still be bending over more than usual from the waist, and this will make the plane of the swing more upright than usual. As a result, you can count on the ball flying in a left-to-right pattern. Accordingly, you should aim a little to the left of the target to compensate.

The watchword during the swing is not to swing too hard. You want to remain steady over the ball in order to make clean contact. One of the best ways to help yourself is to think of maintaining the Tilt on both types of sidehill lies. Obviously, any change in the Tilt during the swing will be disastrous.

The key thought for these uneven lies is not to swing at too fast a tempo. We'll put it even more strongly: Never swing with your full power from these lies. Swing a little "softer" than usual and take plenty of club (except of course on downhill lies), and soon you will find yourself contacting the ball flush and generally enjoying the satisfaction of playing these challenging shots well.

OBITZ AND FARLEY SAY:

1. In order to be a good shotmaker, you've got to be a good swinger. The different swings are what make the shots for you, and the good swinger can vary his swing to meet the situation.

2. To land the ball on the green with plenty of backspin or with less backspin is a matter of learning to vary the swing tempo. To vary the tempo, you vary the tempo at which the arms swing; the body responds with the appropriate timing. The best way to learn this is to practice hitting the ball different distances with the same length of swing.

3. There are basically two methods of curving the ball left and right and hitting it high and low. The first method involves changes in the setup; the second, modifications of the swing. You should pick the method that suits your skills—or combine the two, if you wish.

4. As a general rule, the more deeply the ball lies in the rough, the firmer you should hold the club and the more "body" you must put into the swing.

5. On uphill, downhill, and sidehill lies, the key thought is not to swing too hard. With an easier swing than normal you can keep your balance far more easily.

9

Sand Play Made Simple

WHEN YOUR BALL LIES in a bunker, the main objective is to get it out. Yet to see the average golfer going about getting his ball out of a bunker, you might well think he was determined to stay in it forever! The main reason he fails to extricate himself the first time is that he doesn't know the correct techniques and will insist on using low-percentage shots.

A golfer goes into a fairway bunker 200 yards from the tee on a 500-yard, par 5 hole. He immediately grabs hold of a 3-wood—after all, this is a par 5 hole and he needs the distance, right?—and puts a big swing on the ball. He loses his balance a little, his feet slide around, and he cold-tops the ball, putting it right up under the lip of the bunker. He could have taken a 5-iron out of the bunker, and then another 5-iron would have put him on the green. There is nothing in the rules that says a par 5 must be played with two woods and a wedge!

Close to the green, it's the same story. The golfer goes into a bunker, and first he tries to beat the system. He takes out a wedge and tries to flick the ball out cleanly. We remember that Walter Hagen could play that shot to perfection, but unfortunately our golfer is no Walter Hagen. He hits the shot a little heavy and it hits the top of the bank and rolls back to his feet. For his next try, he takes a full, wild slash at the ball and the club buries fully six inches behind the ball. The ball rolls a couple of feet—still in the bunker!

Well, the point is made. The average golfer's difficulty with bunkers is that he has no clear idea about how to play them. Let's clear it up once and for all.

Fairway Bunkers

Our example of the average golfer in a fairway bunker was only a slight exaggeration of what commonly happens. The golfer made every mistake he could have. Now let's see what should be done.

The first thing to check in a fairway bunker is the lie. If the lie is good, you can consider going for distance. But if the ball is partially or completely buried in the sand, you must "explode" the ball with a sand wedge, however far you still have to go on the hole.

The second thing to check is the height of the lip of the bunker. If the lip is so high that a 9-iron would not clear it, the answer's obvious: Go to the wedge and "explode" the ball. You're better off anywhere outside the bunker than you are still in the bunker and under the lip. If the lip is lower, you must calculate what club has enough loft for you to clear the lip comfortably.

Only at this point should you take into account the distance you need on the shot. If you approach the shot the other way around and say to yourself, I need such and such a club to get home, you'll find yourself reaching for the same club you would use on the fairway and ignoring both the lie and the height of the lip. As we've seen, this approach doesn't work.

In executing the fairway bunker shot, the first move is to dig in well with your feet. If your feet slip in the sand during the swing, it will ruin the shot. The second move is to choke down slightly on the grip—because you have lowered the level of your feet while the ball is still on the top of the sand. During the swing, the important point is to swing smoothly, your mind made up to take the ball cleanly with the swing— ball first, in other words, then a little sand. To do this, we think it important not to take so big a swing or to swing at such a fast tempo that the left heel rises in the backswing. If the left heel rises, there's a good chance your left foot will slip. Instead, swing flat-footed. This will have the effect of restricting the backswing to about the three-quarter mark and make it easier to maintain a steady "Swing Center."

Coming through the ball, you should emphasize releasing the right side. The last thing you want to do on this shot is to leave your weight on the right side through the hitting area. (This could lead to hitting behind the ball.) It's far better to hit a fairway bunker shot a little thin than any sort of "fat" shot. A slightly thinned shot will always get out of the bunker as long as you have allowed for a margin of safety by selecting a club with just a bit more loft than absolutely necessary. A "fat" shot can leave the ball in the bunker.

The most important point to remember about fairway bunker shots—or any bunker shot for that matter—is that you must not swing *at* the ball, you must swing *through* the ball. We've seen more of these shots missed because the golfer concerned did not make up his mind to make a *complete swing* of it than for any other reason.

Greenside Bunkers

When it comes to greenside bunkers, we think that a lot of golfers are confused by such advice as "close the blade on this shot" and "open the blade on that shot." They are forever trying to make the ball do tricks every time they step into a greenside bunker. In nine cases out of ten, all that is required is a perfectly ordinary, straightforward explosion shot. You must have this basic shot in your bag before you mess around with anything more fancy.

Until you acquire a lot of experience and confidence in your sand play, it is best to standardize your length of swing and vary the distance obtained by varying the distance you strike the sand behind the ball. The length of swing we recommend is the three-quarter swing. You can vary the distance you get by hitting two inches, one inch, and half an inch behind the ball. For maximum distance, you would take the ball first and the sand after, in exactly the same way you would make an iron shot from the fairway.

Before outlining the mechanics of the explosion shot, we would like to talk about the sand wedge. It's very well designed to do its job, though we have found that most golfers don't understand this. Compared to a 9-iron, the sand wedge has more weight, more loft, and a much wider flange. It is also appreciably deeper in the face from top to bottom.

The extra weight of the sand wedge helps you deal with the resistance of the sand. The extra loft makes it easier for you to get the ball up and out of the bunker. And its wide flange means that it will skid through the sand. In contrast, a 9-iron would dig more deeply into the sand. The extra depth on the sand wedge gives a wide margin for error in contacting the ball.

We have taken the trouble to explain this because we still find golfers who don't bother to carry a sand wedge. They make do with a 9-iron or a pitching wedge. This is crazy! (Old-time golfers didn't have a sand wedge; at that time you tried to lay back a niblick—9-iron—and shave out a shallow cut of sand with the ball. Considering the fact that those old niblicks often had a leading edge that was as sharp as a razor, it was a miracle anyone could get out of a bunker at all. In fact, in those days only the best players were good bunker players because of the skill needed to play the shot.) Why handicap yourself by playing the sand shot with a club that makes the shot more difficult? If you're still unconvinced, check the bag of any tournament player. You will find a sand wedge in it, no question at all.

To set up for the explosion shot, take a slightly open stance with the left foot withdrawn slightly from the target line. This will help you swing through the shot. Play the ball off the left heel and remember to keep your stance narrow—your heels should not be more than six inches apart. (A narrow stance will keep you in position "over the ball" to deliver a precision blow. With a wider stance, it becomes possible to sway to the right, and the result of the sway could mean entering the sand too far behind the ball to get it out of the bunker.) As on other shots, keep your right foot at right angles to the target line, but turn your left foot out a little more than normal, to 45 degrees or so. This will help time the shot properly in the downswing and ensure that you finish the shot with a complete follow-through.

Another important factor in the setup is that you take a slightly firmer hold on the club. This will help you swing through the resistance of the sand more easily. It's the same principle as with the rough; if you expect to meet resistance at impact, you should adopt a slightly firmer hold. However, in taking a firmer hold, make certain that the left hand is holding appreciably more firmly than the right. This will prevent the right forearm rolling over the left too soon in the follow-through and possibly closing the blade.

Finally, the clubface should be square to the target line for this particular explosion shot.

The swing for the sand wedge will be more upright than that for any other club because the sand wedge has the shortest length of all the iron clubs, and this dictates that the ball be played close to the body—closer in fact than for any other club. However, the principles we discussed earlier about setting up to the different clubs still apply. You establish the right Tilt for the sand wedge by making certain your wrists are slightly arched. The swing is made in exactly the same fashion we described for the three-quarter swing.

A word about tempo: There must be no chopping at the ball and no stabbing. You must eliminate from your mind the thought that it is necessary to muscle the ball out of the sand. This is a common mental error in sand play; it accounts for a lot of missed sand shots. The swing should be leisurely, a little slower than you would take for a regular 9-iron shot. A very good idea of the correct tempo can be had by watching the best sand players in action. Sam Snead is a wonderful sand player; so is Julius Boros. Both take their time with the sand wedge.

Another characteristic of the best sand players is that they always swing right through the shot—there's no cutting off the finish prematurely. *More sand shots are missed by people swinging to the ball and stopping than for any other reason.* People will insist on stopping their arm swing at the ball! But this stops the clubhead cold and, as a result, the club just buries and there's no force to knock the ball out. Actually, watching the best sand players, it appears that most of the action takes place from the moment the club enters the sand through to the follow-through. This is an illusion, but it indicates the importance of a full finish on the shot.

The club must pass through the ball on all bunker shots to keep the ball on line and to assure its getting out of the bunker. You must definitely think of the sand wedge shot as a cutting action into the sand, under and through the ball. Here are two good images to keep in mind: Imagine that the ball is lying on a dollar bill that is aligned lengthwise at the hole; instead of hitting the ball out of the bunker, think of hitting the whole dollar bill out. Or, think of the ball lying in the middle of a fried egg; again, don't just hit the ball; but hit the whole egg out of the bunker.

Now let's examine more closely what happens to the club and the ball in the impact area. When the club enters the sand two inches behind the ball, the clubhead passes under the ball, with a cushion of sand about three-quarters of an inch thick between the ball and the clubface. Because the flange on the club is about three-quarters of an inch below the ball, the striking force for the blow is limited to the top portion of the blade. This of course gives less distance than when the flange, with its weight, is behind the ball at impact. The heavy flange in this case passes under the ball and gives you a higher trajectory than if you were to play a sand wedge from the fairway.

A large amount of sand between the clubface and the ball means that the grooves on the club never get a grip on the ball. So this type of action will produce no backspin at all. The ball will come out high, drop softly on the green, and roll hardly at all. The result, then, of entering the sand two inches behind the ball is to give you maximum height, minimum backspin, and minimum distance—around 10 yards, depending on the texture of the sand.

By using the same setup and three-quarter swing, you can gain another five yards or so just by entering the sand about one inch behind the ball. When the club enters the sand, it will not be as much below the ball as before. This means that the ball will be struck a little lower on the clubface and more of the weight of the flange will be behind the ball. The trajectory you obtain will be lower than before, there will be more forward driving force than before (hence the extra distance), and you will obtain a little more backspin than with the two-inch shot, although not as much as when the clubhead strikes the sand closer to the ball.

An interesting phenomenon occurs when you strike the sand half an inch behind the ball. There is then only a very thin layer of sand between the clubface and the ball, and this creates a tremendous abrasive action on the ball, resulting in maximum backspin. This is how the experts make the ball bite and dance back from its landing point on the green.

Hitting half an inch behind the ball also means that most of the flange strikes on the back of the ball instead of passing underneath it. The weight of the flange coming in behind the ball will drive it farther than before and on a lower trajectory.

In order to produce maximum distance and lowest trajectory, you contact the ball first and then the sand. Here the backspin is caused by the ball being squeezed between the clubface and the sand in much the same way as when you play an iron shot from the fairway. You obtain a good amount of backspin with this shot, though not as much as when you hit half an inch behind the ball. Here the trajectory of the ball is the lowest of the four shots we've described and the distance the longest, simply because the whole weight of the flange is behind the ball.

So far there has not been a word about altering the length of the standard three-quarter swing. This was quite deliberate. For the less-than-expert golfer it is not desirable to change the swing when you can send the ball the various distances you want simply by changing the distance you hit behind the ball. The formula for this can be expressed

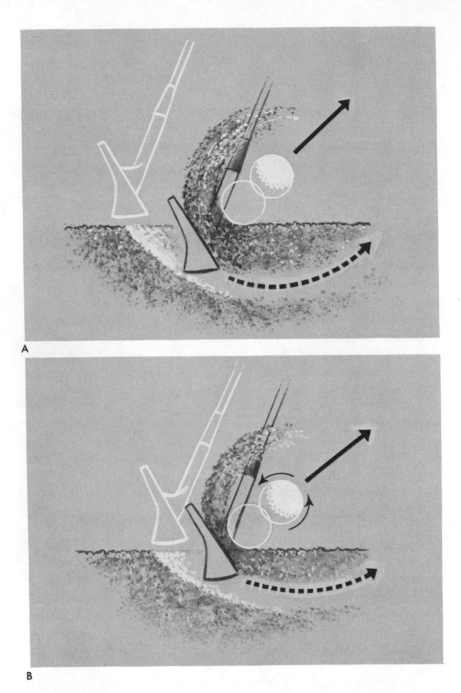

A

B

When the club enters the sand two inches behind the ball (A), you get maximum height, minimum backspin, and minimum distance. When the club enters one inch behind the ball (B), you get a little more backspin and distance and a slightly lower trajectory. When the club enters half an

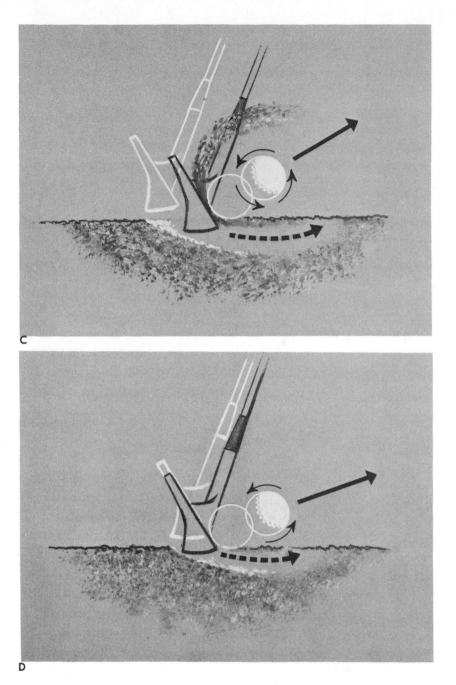

C

D

inch behind (C), you get maximum backspin due to the abrasive action of the thin layer of sand between the clubface and the ball; you get more distance and again a lower trajectory. When you strike the ball first and then the sand (D), you get the lowest trajectory, the maximum distance, and good backspin.

very simply: The farther you hit behind the ball, the more height, the less distance, and the less backspin you obtain. The closer you hit behind the ball, the less height, the more distance, and the more backspin you obtain.

Of course you should realize that there are variations of these shots and that, as you become more experienced, you can try such shots as a half-swing entering the sand at various distances behind the ball. But to learn from scratch to be a good sand player, it's most practical to standardize the length of the swing.

Now we'll discuss two problem lies in the bunker that give the average golfer fits. One is commonly called the "fried-egg" lie; it's a ball buried in a saucer-like depression in the sand. The second occurs when you must get the ball up quickly over the lip of the bunker.

The "Fried-egg" Lie

The "fried-egg" lie strikes terror into the hearts of average golfers. They're convinced that the only way to get the ball out is to use all their physical strength. Wrong! It's just a matter of technique.

To play the "fried egg" lie, close the face of the sand wedge and aim to hit the sand about two inches behind the ball. The ball will come out low and running.

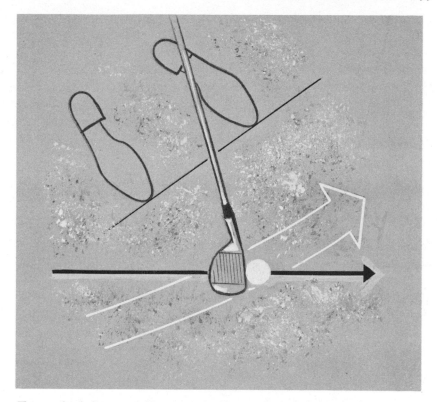

To get the ball up quickly, open the blade and then take your normal hold. Aim the leading edge of the sand iron slightly to the left of the flag, then set up to ball, aligning your body well to the left of target. In the swing, you slice right under the ball, popping the ball out on to the green.

All you have to do is to close the face of the sand wedge slightly and aim to hit the sand about two inches behind the ball. Take the same three-quarter length swing and maintain the same even tempo as before and the ball will come out very easily. What happens is this: Because you have closed the blade of the wedge, it does not skid through the sand as before but instead cuts down through and under the ball. There is increased resistance from the sand in this case, and because of this you firm up the hold a little more than on a regular sand shot. You will find that the ball comes out lower and runs a good distance, so you should allow for this in planning the shot. You will also find that the follow-through you can achieve is shorter than usual. But make a determination to swing through as far as you can, even if it's only two or three feet past the ball. As we've said, more sand shots are failures because of not swinging through the ball than for any other reason.

How to Get the Ball Up Quickly

When you have to get the ball up quickly, what you need to do is to increase the effective loft on the sand wedge. And you do this by opening the blade.

If you see that you need to hit this type of shot, you set the blade open and take your hold while standing outside the bunker. Rest the club on the grass and open the blade. Take your normal hold on the club. Now go into the bunker and aim the leading edge of the sand iron a little to the left of the flag. Set up to the ball, aligning your body well to the left of the hole. Now all you do is make a straightforward three-quarter swing along the line of swing established by your body alignment, aiming to hit the sand about two inches behind the ball. In effect, you are slicing right underneath the ball. The ball will pop up and, because of the slice-spin on the ball, kick a little to the right on landing.

No chapter on sand play would be complete without emphasizing the need for practice. If you want to be a good sand player, there's absolutely no substitute for going into a bunker with a dozen balls at a time and getting acquainted with the principles we've discussed here.

We remember attending the U.S. Open at Winged Foot a few years ago. One evening, after the day's play was over, we watched the pros practice. Several of them took a few minutes to practice their bunker shots, maybe hitting a dozen balls in all. But then along came Gary Player. Gary, as you know, is possibly the greatest sand player of all time. He didn't just hit a dozen balls, or even two dozen. An hour later, when we left, he was still hitting balls out of that practice bunker!

OBITZ AND FARLEY SAY:

1. More sand shots are failures because the player does not swing through to a complete finish than for any other reason.

2. Brute force is not necessary in a bunker. A smooth swing and the proper technique are all that are necessary.

3. Until you acquire a lot of experience and confidence in the sand, it is easiest to hit the explosion shot with a standard three-quarter swing and vary the distance behind the ball at which you have the blade enter the sand (to send the ball the required distance).

10
The Short Game

ONE OF THE BEAUTIES of the Obitz/Farley system of learning golf is that the closer you get to the green the more comfortable you feel. By first learning the quarter-swing and then progressing via the half-swing and the three-quarter swing to the full swing, you have already learned the basic swings of a good short game.

You have already learned that the shorter the swing—applied here, that means the closer you are to the green—the shorter you should hold the club. And the shorter the stroke, the more you should open and narrow your stance. Now we would like to expand a little on these points, in the context of the short game.

If you were going to run the ball from just off the green, you would hold the club right at the bottom of the grip. (On some of these shots, you may even have part of the right hand holding the shaft itself.) If you were 25 yards away from the green, you would move up two or three inches on the grip. And if you were about to play a short runup shot of about 50 yards, you would hold the club about halfway down the grip. The hold in each case would be shorter than in the case of a full swing. Holding the club shorter gives you the necessary precision, rhythm, and timing for these shorter shots because it brings the ball in closer to the body and, consequently, the arm swing is more directly away from the

155

ball and through the ball. It's more of a straight-line swing than in a full swing (where you stand taller to the ball and the swing is necessarily more from the inside).

The open stance side of the short game helps your body time these shorter swings properly. We want to stress the importance of narrowing the stance as you near the green because so many average golfers make the same mistake of adopting too wide a stance. This has two undesirable effects: It allows too broad a range of ball positions and it permits or makes probable too much use of the upper body (heaving and jerking at the ball with the big muscles of the upper arms and shoulders). In a narrow stance, the bottom of the swing arc is confined to a narrow area between the feet. You can swing with precision, and the closer your feet are together the less chance there will be that the big muscles of the upper body will get into the act. The narrower stance helps you stay over the ball, makes you play the shot more with the arm swing, and gives you greater sensitivity in the hands for feel. (If you find any of this unclear, review the section on the "feet together" swing on page 89; it all ties in together.)

The basic shot you will use in the short game, between a full swing with a wedge and chipping distance of the green, is the pitch shot. The pitch shot flies high, lands near the pin, and stops with a good deal of backspin. To get the height you need, you would normally select a pitching wedge for this shot. However, to get a slightly lower shot (say, into a wind), you can play the same shot and get a lower flight by using a 9-iron. If you need extra height, you can pitch with the sand wedge. About the only restrictions are that you should only use a sand wedge when you have a good lie (off a tight lie its slightly rounded sole could lead to a bladed shot) and that, because of the weight of the club and the fact that most of that weight is in the sole, there's a limit to how far you can hit the sand wedge without the sole's skidding right underneath the ball and sending it higher but not farther. Learn your own *comfortable* maximum distance with your sand wedge and never select it for a shot of greater distance than that maximum.

To play the pitch shot, set up with a narrow, open stance—how narrow and how open will depend on the length of the swing—and position the ball just back of the left heel. You should position your hands over the ball or slightly *ahead* of the ball so that you can catch the ball with a slightly descending blow. However, never position the hands behind the ball; this can lead to the clubhead's getting ahead of the hands through the hit, causing an undesirable "scooping" action.

The swing is exactly as you learned it; it can vary from a mini-swing to three-quarter length. However, even a comparatively inexperienced golfer can make simple variations on this basic swing to get a desired result. You might initially experiment with the ball position. Playing the ball forward, off the left instep, will result in a slightly higher trajectory. Playing the ball back in the stance, say a couple of inches to the right of the left heel, will result in a slightly lower shot.

Once you've mastered ball position, work in a little change of tempo. (Here you can refer to the section on varying the tempo of the swing [see page 128] and apply this to various lengths of swing.) The purpose here, of course, is to learn how to land the ball on the green with plenty of backspin or with less backspin.

Speaking of the shotmaking chapter, we should add that working the ball to the left and right is also a part of the complete short game. And the relevant portions of that chapter do apply. However, this is advanced golf. If you're a 5-handicap or better, by all means practice these shots; if you're not, you should leave them alone.

Any golfer who has learned the basic swing can and should learn the shots we will describe now. So many amateurs we play with are what we call "one shot" golfers. They know the pitch shot and the chip shot and little else. If you put the following shots into your bag—and there's only one way to do that, through practice—you will have the shots you need for just about every occasion.

The Punch Shot

The punch shot is designed to fly low and to hold its line beautifully. It's therefore a great shot on windy days (especially into the wind). It's also useful for getting out of the rough, as it is made primarily with the arm swing and shoulder action.

To set up for the punch shot, put extra weight on the left foot. Instead of the normal 50–50 distribution of weight between the feet, you want to feel that about 70 percent of your weight is on the left foot. The ball is played farther back toward the right foot than usual; this will position the hands ahead of the ball. The hold on the club is extra firm in both hands in the setup and throughout the swing. With a firm hold, you will have less wrist action—and this eliminates any chance of "flicking" the ball and flying it high in the air.

During the swing, it's important to swing back just to three-quarter length so that you can keep your weight on the left foot. Since you don't come off the left foot, you get a tighter coiling action on the backswing,

To play the punch shot, Harry Obitz plays the ball back in the stance, with 70 percent of the weight on the left foot. The hold should be extra firm for this shot. Swing back to three-quarter-length only (A), and keep the left arm and wrist firm right into the finish. This ensures that the body follows the shot more than normal (B).

and the right side will release more strongly going through the ball. (It's really the same action we discussed earlier in playing the rough. If you firm up the hold, you get less wrist action, and therefore there must be more body action than usual to time the blade into the ball.) It's essential to the success of the shot that you keep the left arm straight and the left wrist firm, as well as the right, through to the finish. This ensures that the body follows the shot more than usual and that the right hand and forearm remain under the shaft (there should be very little or no climbover of the right hand and forearm over the left). If you play the shot right, the club and the arms will point straight to the hole in the finish and the right side will be completely released.

The Flick Shot

The flick shot is right at the opposite end of the shotmaking spectrum from the punch shot. Here you're looking for a lot of wrist action, so you hold the club very lightly. (We hope you realize that there is a very simple correlation between the pressure in the hold and wrist action: The firmer the hold, the less wrist action you get; the lighter the hold, the more wrist action you get.)

The chief use of the flick shot is in hitting up to an elevated green. The ball will fly very high, and the only limitation on the shot is distance. Because primarily you're using the arms and wrists to make the shot, you must find your own comfortable maximum with this shot— and stay within it at all times. Another caution: This shot always needs a good lie.

To set up for the flick shot, adopt a narrow stance with the ball a little back from the left heel. Hold the club lightly in the fingers with equal pressure in both hands. In playing the shot, swing the club back with the forearms, allowing plenty of freedom in the wrists and permitting the right arm to stay very close to the right side going back and allowing the left arm to fold quickly and return to the left side in the follow-through. This is a very narrow swing and, although you should not consciously use the wrists, you should permit them to cock and uncock very freely. The shot will *feel* very "wristy" even though this is a result, not a cause. There should be only enough shoulder and body action to time the swing properly. However, if you just permit the shoulders and body to respond as on a normal swing, they will respond in the correct amount. There's more body drive than normal in the punch shot, less body drive than normal in the flick shot.

For Advanced Golfers Only. The flick shot can be useful for applying hook-spin and slice-spin so that you can work the ball toward the pin when the green contour is favorable. To apply slice-spin, you would open the stance more, play the ball a little more forward in the stance, and swing back outside the target line a little, keeping the club-face open throughout the swing. To keep the clubface open going through the ball, you would lead a little longer than normal with the left arm. For hook-spin, you would close the stance a little, close the blade a little, and play the ball a little farther back in the stance. You would swing back inside the target line a little more than usual, keeping the clubface closed and making a little freer turn with the shoulders than on the slice-spin shot. Coming through the ball, you would let the right hand and forearm climb over the left a little before impact, thus assuring that the clubface is closed a little at impact.

The Stop Shot

Dick Farley learned this shot when growing up with Ken Venturi in California. Ken became so skilled with this shot that he could nominate in advance of the shot how many times the ball would bounce before it spun to a stop! This shot flies low with superior backspin due to a more vertical attack on the ball than usual. It will give you the finest ball control possible from any lie, and it's also the best shot from a tight lie.

In the setup the stance is square and the ball is positioned right of center and back toward the right foot. You should flex the knees inward slightly toward each other, and you should have about 60 percent of your weight on the left foot. Hold very firmly with the last three fingers of the left hand throughout the shot. To provide the sharply vertical backswing, position the right elbow close into your right side in the set and keep it close to the body as you swing back. Otherwise the back-swing is normal—the clubface is kept in a square position and there is a full arm swing and shoulder turn. The most important aspect of the shot is that the left side must lead the shoulders and arms into the downswing. You achieve this by *sliding* the knees to the left to initiate the downward movement. The other important point is to keep your chin pointed at the ball until after impact; this will keep your head behind the ball.

To play the flick shot, Harry Obitz sets up with a narrow stance, holding the club very lightly in both hands. In playing the shot, you should allow plenty of freedom in the wrists and only enough shoulder and body action to time the action properly (A and B).

To play the stop shot, Dick Farley sets up with the ball back in the stance and about 60 percent of the weight on the left foot. To achieve the necessary vertical backswing, you position the right elbow close to the right side in the set and keep it close to the body as you swing back (A). The key to the success of the shot is to initiate the downswing with a sliding action of the knees to the left; this ensures a steep downward swing through the ball (B).

The Lob Shot

The lob shot is a high-trajectory shot that can be played from the rough or where you need to carry the ball over an obstacle such as a tree or bunker. It has little backspin but, because the ball descends almost vertically onto the green, it will roll very little. You need at least a fair lie to play this shot.

To set up for the lob shot, stand tall to the ball with the ball positioned a little closer to the body than on a normal pitch shot. The ball should be forward in the stance, more off the instep of the left foot, rather than just back of the heel. The hold on the club should be light but not loose; you should weaken the hold a little on this shot, that is, turn your hands a little to the left of their normal, square position on the club. Set up with a little more weight on the right foot than the left.

The main thing in the lob shot is to be sure to take a long back-swing. This enables you to use just the weight of the arms and club to swing through the ball. You swing back with a long, leisurely action and then just allow the weight of the arms and the club to "drop" through the ball. You don't accelerate the arm swing as you would on a normal pitch shot. During the backswing, the clubface is gradually opened by the hands.

When practicing this shot, check that you have opened the hands by seeing that both wrists are under the shaft at the top of the swing. In the downswing, delay the weight transfer to the left foot by keeping your right heel down until the ball is struck. To ensure maximum height, delay the right hand's climbing over the left until the ball is well on its way.

A variation on the lob shot, the "cut lob" shot, is useful when you need extra stop on the shot. Here you face left of the hole with the body and aim the leading edge of the blade at the hole. The swing is exactly the same as that for the lob shot. However, because the clubface is open in relation to the body alignment and therefore the line of the swing, you cut across the ball, imparting enough sidespin to stop the ball very quickly.

The Runup Shot

The runup shot is seldom seen in this country, but in Britain they use it all the time. As its name implies, this shot is one in which the ball is kept low and rolls the majority of the distance to the hole. On the seaside courses in Britain, where the fairway turf is firm and very true, it

To play the lob shot, Dick Farley sets up with the ball forward in the stance, and a little more weight on the right foot than the left. The main point is to take a long, leisurely swing (A), so that you can then just allow the weight of the arms and club to "drop" through the ball (B).

makes sense to run the ball up to the hole even from a distance as long as 100 yards—especially when you're faced with a 30-mile-per-hour headwind or sidewind! In America we normally need to carry the ball onto the green because, with our conditions, bouncing the ball short of the green is undependable.

However, there can be circumstances where it would be useful to have the runup in your bag. One of these is a desperation shot out from under trees where elevation on the shot is out of the question. And some public courses, not watered as much as private courses, may have conditions in which the fairways are hard and the greens too hard to hold a pitch shot. Here running the ball up can make a lot of sense. Third, a short version of the runup can be very useful close to the green, when you have to chip the ball to a two-tier green, from the lower level to the top level, or where the green is heavily contoured. It is much easier to run a ball onto a green with severe left or right breaks; a pitched ball will exaggerate the amount of break and leave you wide of the hole.

Playing the runup shot is primarily a matter of intelligent club selection. You need a 4-iron or a 5-iron for the shot; anything more lofted will send the ball too high. You should put a little more weight on your left foot than you would in a normal quarter-swing or half-swing, and you should firm up your hold on the club. Otherwise, it is a normal swing. In essence, you play the runup in the same way you would a punch shot; the only difference, really, is in the length of the swing and club selection.

Chip Shots

From one point of view, chip shots are little quarter-swings that you play around from just off the green. However, they do deserve a few words by themselves.

Undoubtedly the most common fault we see in chipping is being too wristy. This fault stems, of course, from holding the club too lightly, and it results in all sorts of mishits—scooping the ball, thin shots, and outright topped shots. You don't have to hold the club so firmly that you become wooden; just hold the club firmly enough to prevent excessive wrist action.

The second type of fault is poor posture in the setup for the chip. (We're talking about points already explained in this chapter: too wide a stance, too long a hold on the club, having the hands behind the ball.)

The setup for the chip should find you with a narrow stance—feet no more than six inches or so apart—an open stance, your right hand down at the bottom of the grip or even on the shaft, and your hands ahead of the ball.

In the swing for the chip shot, one of the more common errors is to turn the shoulders as the first move. When you do that, you take the club back to the inside too quickly, which makes it extremely difficult to hit the ball straight. Instead, these shots should be made primarily with the arm swing, with just enough shoulder and body action to blend the action. In this way you will keep the swing more on line.

Intelligent club selection is vital for good chip shots. We remember playing nine holes on one occasion with one of our professionals. At the end of the round he was dissatisfied with his game around the green. He had just missed five greens and had taken three shots to get down each time. We told him that he had misclubbed himself—he had used a wedge for all these shots, and it just wasn't necessary. To prove our point, we took him out to the practice green. He brought his wedge and we brought our 5-irons. We got inside him every time—for the reason that one time he would stub the wedge and come up short and the next time overcompensate and hit too far.

We don't say it's impossible to chip with a wedge. We're saying that, if you're just off the green, it's far easier to chip with a 5-, 6- or 7-iron than a more lofted club, because with a lofted club you have to hit the ball perfectly to get the result you want. With a 5-, 6- or 7-iron you can mishit the ball and still come up with an acceptable result.

You can use a 5-iron up to about five yards off the green. When you're farther out than that you may need to go to a 7-iron to carry the ball onto the green. Leave chipping with wedges to those few experts who have mastered it; it's too difficult for the average golfer.

We'll conclude this chapter with a thought on developing touch. People will say that either you're born with good touch or you're not. We don't believe that, and we suspect that those who say it are people who have tried to develop touch the wrong way. We're forever seeing people practice their chipping with a 9-iron or a wedge. When you do that, it may feel easy—but out on the course, you'll stick your club in the ground!

Instead, those chip shots you would normally play on the course with a 5-iron should be practiced with a 4-iron. The ball moves so quickly off a 4-iron that you rapidly develop a really nice stroke. You'll find that this helps your touch when you're on the course and actually

using the 5-iron. And the same thing applies to those chips you would normally play with a 7-iron on the course: Play them with a 5-iron. We assure you that if you practice your chip shots this way, you will soon develop both a good stroke and good touch.

OBITZ AND FARLEY SAY:

1. Don't be a "one shot" golfer in the short game. You need a battery of shots to turn three shots into two consistently.

2. The primary causes of poor chipping are a poor setup and making too "wristy" a stroke.

3. Learn to chip with several clubs. "One club" chippers are usually bad chippers.

4. To develop touch around the green, always practice with a less lofted club than the one you would use on the course.

11
Putting Is Not a Different Game

ONE OF THE OLDEST CLICHÉS in golf is that golf and putting are two different games. People say, Golf is a game where the ball flies in the air, and putting is a game where the ball rolls on the ground. While the golf swing can be taught, they believe, no one can teach you a thing about putting. They say you're on your own when it comes to putting—or that any old style of putting is fine as long as the ball goes into the hole.

Such attitudes are not just negative, they're wrong! The first clue to this is that many of the fine swingers have also been fine putters: Mac Smith was one of the finest swingers ever of the golf club and he was as good a putter as any. Bobby Jones was a beautiful swinger *and* a beautiful putter. Horton Smith was known as a great putter—but he also had a great swing. Lloyd Mangrum was the same. And today two of the finest swingers in the game, Jack Nicklaus and Johnny Miller, are both superb putters.

The reason these fine swingers were and are fine putters is a simple one: *They swing the putter!* They don't pick up the putter with their wrists and bang down on the ball. They don't lift the putter with their arms and shoulders and heave at the ball. The putting swing will be smaller than the one you use even for a quarter-stroke, but it's still a swing.

Our pupils never have the problem of trying to learn a different game on the putting green. We start them with the quarter-swing with the 7-iron and the "brushing" technique. And during the first lesson, we will also take them to the putting green. Once they have the idea of brushing back and brushing through on the fairway, and have hit a few shots with the brushing action, they can learn to do the same sort of thing on the shorter grass of the putting green.

We'll start them perhaps a foot from the hole, where they only have to brush back maybe a couple of inches and through a couple of inches. Then we'll take them a little farther from the hole, again they'll brush back and through, and before you know it they're swinging the putter very nicely. For people who have not been inhibited by years of playing and confused by different theories of putting, it's a very simple move to brush the putting surface. We find that even experienced golfers can learn the putting swing by brushing, so long as they will give it an honest try. If you're brushing back and through, you can't be jerking, lifting, or shoving the blade—you are forced to swing it!

We gradually move our pupil farther and farther from the hole with the brushing technique. When we get to the edge of the green we put a ball down on the fringe and a 5-iron in his hand, and we have him choke down on it and chip the ball with the "brush." Our pupil realizes immediately that the only difference between putting and the rest of the game is the length of the swing and the loft of the club. The same brushing technique which induces the true swing will serve him well wherever he is on the golf course.

This is perhaps one of the most important discoveries the pupil will make about the game. Later, when pupils are swinging with longer clubs and full swings, you can always take them back to brushing the grass with the putter or a chip shot and immediately they will know where the club should be and what it should be doing in the impact area. For example, a pupil will graduate to the 2-iron, and he tries to force it. And you can say to him, "Look, you don't force the 5-iron." And the pupil will reply, "No, that's right, I'm a good 5-iron player." You ask, "Why is that?" And either he says or you can explain that the reason is that on the 5-iron, you are using the brushing, swinging technique. Right away, the pupil gets the idea that he was just not swinging the 2-iron. We think it is important for the pupil to have an easy way of putting his game back together when things go wrong, and "brushing" does the job every time.

In putting, another point we make is that the first principle of a golf swing—and putting in particular—is that the ball is round and has weight. If it's rolling downhill, it will practically roll by itself; the fact that it is round and has weight will carry it down the hill. If you are putting uphill, the reverse will be true. The ball's weight works against you, and you will have to make a longer swing to get the ball up to the hole. Here's one illustration of this: If you went to the top of a kiddies' slide and put the ball down on the top of the incline, it would roll on down to the bottom and shoot off. However, if you set the ball at the bottom of the slide, you would have to make a great effort to roll it to the top.

When reading a putt, you have to think in terms of how much effort—how forceful a swing—you need to move this amount of weight (the ball), remembering that it is "rolling" weight. When you think in this way, you are thinking in terms of *rolling* the ball rather than belting it or jerking it. Rolling the ball means simply this: If you truly swing a putter at and through the ball, you will start it rolling properly. But if you jerk at the ball, or cut across it, it will skid across the green.

Once our pupils understand the principle of "rolling" weight, we have them practice reading the line of a putt. They put down a ball on the practice green and read the putt to one hole, then we have them move around the ball and read the putt to another hole, and so on. This type of practice is useful at all times in your career. Whenever you practice your putting, always spend a few minutes practicing your reading of putts. You will soon appreciate that the weight of the rolling ball is really the factor you must think about, whether the putt is uphill, downhill, or there is a break from one side or the other.

We've just spoken of "reading the line of a putt." We used that expression because it is in common use, but you would never hear us use it in our own teaching. Most weekend golfers pick out the "line" to the hole, set the putter blade down at right angles to the "line," and try to roll the putt down the "line" to the hole. Since the line is wafer thin, the golfer is apt to imagine that if he deviates a fraction of an inch to the right or left, he won't hole the putt. In his anxiety to keep his putt on "line" he often tenses up and fails to swing the putter properly.

We advocate putting along a "track" to the hole. This track will be four and a quarter inches wide. Get down behind the ball and determine the direction and speed of the putt. Then set the putter down at a right angle to the direction of the putt and sight from the toe of the putter to the right side of the hole and from the heel to the left side of the hole. This will create in your mind the image of the four-and-a-quarter-inch track because the putter blade is usually the same length from toe to heel as the width of the hole.

Putting down the track will give you a lot of confidence. In making the putt, it will seem to you very easy to keep the ball between the two lines. And putting down the "track" is easier than putting along a thin, scary line!

In our own game, after many years of using the "track" method of visualizing the path of the putt, we can get a clear image of the track on even the longest, most breaking putt. However, you may have difficulty initially in visualizing the track, especially on longer putts. We suggest that you start working with the track on shorter putts—say, six- to eight-footers—and gradually progress to longer putts. You will soon be able to visualize the track on medium putts of up to 20 feet. If, though, try as you may, you can't see the track on those long putts, then give up! Visualize the track for the first 10 feet or so of the putt and stroke the ball along the shortened track at the appropriate speed.

If you have difficulty visualizing the track on any length of putt, you should use your imagination a little more strongly. You will have to develop your own way of "seeing" it. Some players, we have found, relate immediately to the word "track," but others prefer to think of a "trough" or a "channel"—and some even erect imaginary "walls" on either side of the track to keep the ball on the track. One of our pupils liked to color the track gold, and maybe that was appropriate, for he won a lot of Nassaus with the method. Whatever you do, don't think about putting down a "line" again!

More advanced players should realize that when we say that the putting stroke must be a swing, we are not saying that there is only one way to putt. Far from it; there is always latitude in golf—and in the swing—for individuality. As the swing gets shorter as you approach the hole, the more difficult it becomes to feel in your fingers the centrifugal force generated in the club (the shorter the swing, the less the centrifugal force). Different golfers will therefore want to feel the putter swing in different ways.

Some golfers prefer to use principally their forearms and wrists, with just a little shoulder action on longer putts. Some golfers prefer to use more arm and shoulder action on every putt and less, and sometimes very little, wrist. Your choice between these two basic styles of putting swing will depend on how firmly you like to hold the putter. If you like to hold the putter lightly, you'll get a lot of wrist action, and you'll be what we call a "forearm-wrist" putter. If you prefer to hold the putter more firmly, you'll get less wrist action, and, to obtain the required distance, you'll need more arm action and responding movement from the shoulders. You are what we call an "arm-shoulder" putter.

These two basic putting styles relate to what we taught you about

If you hold the putter very lightly, you'll get a lot of wrist action, and you'll be a "forearm-wrist" putter (A and B). If you hold the putter more firmly, you'll get less wrist action, and to obtain the required distance, you'll need more arm and shoulder action; you'll then be an "arm-shoulder" putter (C and D).

the swing in our discussion of the short game, when we dealt with the flick and punch shots. In the flick shot, you held lightly to obtain plenty of wrist action and, when you did that, you needed less body action. In the punch shot, where you held firmly, you got less wrist action and needed more body action. It all comes back to the two basic working parts of the swing: The arms make the swing and the body times the swing. This is true no matter what type of swing you make—a full swing, a putting swing, or any special swing.

At this point some of our readers may want to know how we explain such putting styles as that used by Gary Player. He "taps" putts. This may be more a question of semantics than anything else. There have been many great putters who "tapped" shots: Bobby Locke, Billy Casper, Bob Rosburg, and Doug Ford, as well as Gary. We would explain it this way: Everyone who is a great putter swings the putter; what the "tap" putter does is to stop the arm swing after the ball is struck. The important thing about swinging the putter is that it must swing at the bottom of the stroke, through contact with the ball, so that the ball starts rolling properly. And the great "tap" putters do that.

Our own individual preference is to swing the putter through to a full finish. But the "tap" putters have proven that a full follow-through is not essential on a putt. What is essential is that the putter truly swings and that the characteristics of a true swinging action are present in your putting stroke (with the exception noted above). For example, you must swing inside-to-square-to-inside on a putt just as much as you should on a regular full swing. Cutting a putt is just as bad as cutting a drive—in both cases you will put undesirable slice-spin on the ball.

There's no essential difference between the putting swing and the full swing. Even on the putting green, "The Swing's the Thing!"

OBITZ AND FARLEY SAY:

1. Putting is not a different game from the rest of golf. Whether you're driving the ball or putting the ball, the swing is all-important.

2. You don't read the "line" of a putt. You should visualize and putt down the "track."

3. There are two basic styles of putting, the "forearm-wrist" style and the "arm-shoulder" style. Both are swings.

12
Practice and Play

WE HAVE DEVOTED practically the whole of this book to the true swing in all its variations from green to tee. But no book on golf would be complete without saying something about the mental side of the game and about how you should plan your own growth as a golfer.

To do this, you must understand that there are (or should be) two sides to every golfer: There's the practicer, and there's the player. Appreciating this distinction is crucial to your progress as a golfer.

Let's follow a typical group of amateur golfers on their weekend round. On the first tee, one player slices a ball into the rough. His friends jump in with all sorts of advice: You pulled across it, says one. You swayed forward, says another. And you bent your left arm, says the third. That golfer's round is probably ruined before it ever got started. He will be thinking now of correcting his swing in one way or another instead of keeping his mind on the game. He has forgotten that he is on the course and not the practice ground.

The practice ground is at once your classroom, your laboratory, and your repair shop. The course is where you play the game to the best of your present ability. Now let's consider these thoughts in more detail.

Practice and Your Goals

The practice ground is your classroom because it is here that you should learn and practice the swing. It is your laboratory because it is here that you should experiment; it is here that you should learn shot-making. It's your repair shop because it is here that you should work out any fault that has crept into the swing.

This leads us to perhaps the most important point about practicing: You must always have a purpose in any practice you do. Otherwise, you are just spinning your wheels.

Go to any practice tee or driving range in your neighborhood and watch amateurs at what they call "practice." You will soon see the force of our observation. The golfers bang out balls, invariably with a driver, and when they slice one ball, they quickly tee up another—and slice again! They seem to believe that if they hit enough balls they will acquire a golf swing somewhere along the way. And that's true; they will acquire some sort of golf action. But it will never be the true swing.

We don't plan to repeat here material we've given you earlier—and we've given you more than enough to enable you to develop your swing, to learn the various shots, and to correct any fault in your swing. What we will do here is suggest ways in which you can set your own goals and give you some pointers on methods of practice.

In order to be able to set realistic goals for yourself as a golfer, you must know at all times how you stand with the game. This means that you must evaluate honestly your strengths and weaknesses. Only from this analysis can you plan your practice—and your play.

The first way to analyze yourself is through study of your rounds. After every round you should take the time to record in your notebook such vital statistics as fairways hit, number of chip shots and sand shots, number of putts, and greens hit in regulation figures. ("Regulation figures" is the number of strokes needed to reach the green, considering the par for the hole and allowing two putts per green. On a par 3 hole, for example, hitting the green "in regulation" means hitting your first shot onto the green; on a par 4 hole, your second shot; and on a par 5 hole, your third shot.) When you review this data, you will discover the part or parts of your game that need work.

If you hit only two fairways and six greens in regulation, your swing needs work. If you hit a high number of greens in regulation but you took 38 or 39 putts per round (par is 36) then either your irons need work or your putting needs work—and possibly both! The point is that such analysis gives you specific things to practice.

Another way to analyze your game is to use what might be called visual aids, anything from a full-length mirror to a TV-replay machine.

Surely just about every house in this country has one full-length mirror. Yet few golfers avail themselves of this very practical aid. You can check your hold, your set, you can even check your alignment in a mirror, and it won't cost you a penny.

A second useful visual aid is the photo. It's surprising how many golfers have never seen themselves swing, yet just about every golfer has a camera of some sort. If you have a movie camera in the house and have never taken a movie of your swing, shame on you! Load up and film yourself!

Basically, you need two views for an analysis of your swing. The first should be from in front of the golfer. If your alignment is square and you're playing the ball off the left heel, the cameraman should shoot right down a line from the ball to the left heel. The second view should be from a point looking at the golfer from the side and down toward the target. Here the cameraman should shoot down the foot line, that is, on a line across the toes parallel to the target line.

We firmly believe in the value of photos, and we use them in our golf schools. We don't use movies, but we do use something just as good: A sequence camera that gives us eight pictures of the swing on an instant film so that we can immediately analyze the pupil's swing.

This leads us to the next point: You can use just about any type of still camera to obtain a sequence of your swing, provided it has a shutter speed of at least 1/100 of a second. (Of course use a faster shutter speed if your camera has it.) The secret is to take enough pictures from the same viewpoint while the golfer continues to hit balls.

TV-replay machines are usually beyond the means of the individual. Many of the better teaching professionals are using them today, however, and with a little effort you can probably find a golf professional in your area who has one. Their chief merit is that you can see the entire swing immediately.

Whatever the medium, when you see your swing for the first time, you may be in for a surprise! Your first reaction may well be, That can't be me! It *is* you, though, and that is the whole point. It gives you a chance to be really objective about your swing and the need to work on whatever flaws you may see.

Now a couple of pointers on practice ground methods: The mistake we see most often is that of hitting a lot of balls rapidly in succession. Dick Farley remembers a conversation he had with Byron Nelson on this very point. Byron said, and we agree, you must avoid firing off balls one after the other. That way you don't have time to think; before you know it you have forgotten what it is you're working on! Each shot should be played as deliberately as though it were during a round. You should sight the target, align yourself properly, and go through your regular countdown pattern. Only then will you be practicing with proper concentration.

The mention of "target" brings up the other point. Too many golfers practice without hitting to a target. Such practice is almost value-less, since you cannot truly analyze the swing you've made unless you know what the target was. Another point about playing to a target: When you practice with your irons, it is a good idea to have a specific target, such as a marker on the range (or a specific tree if there are no markers). With irons you need accuracy. However, when you practice with the woods, never try to hit toward a tree or to any one point. For the average golfer, a specific target is far too demanding. All it will make you do is tighten up to the point where you lose your freedom of swing.

Instead, pick out two trees at least 25 to 30 yards apart and practice trying to land the ball in between them. Here you have a target for your woods that is roughly fairway width, a realistic target. If you become really good with your woods, by all means practice keeping one drive on the right side of your "fairway" and the next on the left side. Then try to split the middle. You'll still be working with the same kind of target you'd face out on the course.

When it comes to putting practice, we find again that the average golfer goes about it in an aimless way. In the same way that it's of no value to bash one ball thoughtlessly after another on the practice ground, it makes little sense just to putt a couple of balls around a practice green.

Here is a method that we have found satisfactory: Make a circle six feet in diameter around a hole. (If you place your putter head in the hole, the other end will lie on the circumference of the circle.) You can't actually paint a circle around the hole, but you can have half a dozen old balls painted, say, red and use them to mark the circle.

Take four balls and scatter them about 18 inches away from the hole. Now putt them all into the hole. If you miss one, start over again until you hole all four in succession. Then place the balls at random at the edge of the circle and putt them all in. If you miss one, start over. This procedure builds confidence in your ability to hole any short but missable putt. When you can do this routine three times without miss-ing a ball, you're ready to practice the long putts.

Set up your six-foot circle, move back 20 feet or more, and again throw the balls down at random. Now step up to each ball in turn and concentrate on just hitting it into the circle. The rationale here is that, once you can hole anything within three feet, then, in a sense, you don't have to get the ball any closer than three feet on the first putt, because you *know* that you can hole the second putt.

You'll soon find that, without your even trying, one or more of the four balls will go right into the hole. The reason for that is simple, too. A circle six feet in diameter is a much bigger target than one merely four and a quarter inches in diameter (the hole). When you practice aiming at the hole from a long distance, it's like trying to hit that tree with a driver—it tightens you up to the extent that you lose the freedom in your putting swing. Aiming for the circle, however, frees you to make a good, free swing.

Before leaving the subject of practice, we'll remind you that practice doesn't always have to be a solo effort. It can also be competitive. We remember practicing some years ago with a dear friend of ours, Helen Stetson, a national champion and a member of our club. We used to go out with her and play around the 18th green with just a couple of clubs each. We would play for 25 cents closest to the hole, 50 cents for "sinks," and a dollar for "drains." (If one person sunk a ball and another sunk right on top, the second player got the dollar.) We used to play that little game for an hour and a half, three days a week, and our short games were never sharper!

Playing the Game

When you go out to play a round, you must take off your "practice" hat and leave it in your locker. You put on your "player" hat, and you don't take it off until the last putt of the round is sunk.

If you watch your favorite professional at a tournament, you'll find that he arrives at least an hour before his starting time. He uses that hour to go out to the practice ground and go through his bag, hitting one or two shots or more with each club. You will also find that he starts by hitting little wedge shots and progresses to the short irons and through the middle irons to the long irons. Then he'll hit a few fairway woods and drives. Finally, he'll go over to the practice green and hit a few putts.

This is a fine procedure, make no mistake about it. A lot of people would call this "practice," and they'd be wrong. The man has not been "practicing," he has been *preparing for the round.*

Many amateurs make the mistake of thinking that the pros "practice" before a round—and so, before their own rounds, they go to the practice ground with the wrong purpose in mind. They practice, they *really* practice. They find they're cutting the ball a little and they try to correct it. They try to learn a new swing in the short time they have, or they try to find their old one. But this is the wrong time for such an effort; you should practice *between* rounds. Before a round, the objective is quite different.

You should be warming up for the round. You warm up your golf muscles and you accustom your mind to the fact that for the next few hours you will be playing golf. You warm up your golf "thinking," too, and this is very important.

If you have time to go through the full procedure of the touring professional, then you should do that. If you don't, cut it down a little; hit a couple of shots with each key club in your bag (wedge, 7-iron, 5-iron, 3-iron, 4-wood, and driver). And if you haven't time for that, the least you can do is to take a couple of clubs and swing them a few times to limber up. Playing without a warmup makes no sense. It can easily take the average golfer four or five holes to get going, and by then the round can be ruined.

The other important aspect of preparation for the round is planning your round. You should mentally play the round beforehand and decide such things as where it will be safe to go strong off the tee and where you will just keep the ball in play. You run through the scorecard in your mind, decide what holes are par holes, what holes are birdie holes, and what holes are bogey holes, and you plan accordingly.

There's no standard plan of attack, because everyone has different abilities. However, the first thought you should have in drawing up your game plan is to be humble, to recognize your true ability at the present moment. If you're a 90-shooter, then that should be your goal for today. If you want to break 90, you should look the course over in your mind and find the holes where you'll have a better chance to improve on your normal play. One thing: A good master plan will always call for keeping the ball in play rather than taking risks. Leave risks to the people with the ability to take them!

When you step on that first tee, remember you came to play the game. It's like taking an examination. It's too late to cram now—you've got to go with the swing and the game you have in your bag. Above all, don't do your practice on the course.

What should you think about? Just sticking to your game plan and playing each shot as it comes. Golf is a game that is played shot by shot and hole by hole, whether you're playing match or stroke play. Remember, there is only one important shot—the next one! What you did on the last shot doesn't matter, and what you're going to do on the following one doesn't matter. Concentrate all your energies on the shot at hand.

Here are some general points on playing the game this way:

1. Make up your mind that you're going to do the very best you can on each shot. Many a match has been lost or a round ruined by a "don't care" shot.

2. Play for position on every shot. Except in holing out, every shot should be planned with the purpose of setting up the next one.

3. Play the shot you know you can make, not the fancy shot you've never practiced.

In playing each shot, you have to realize that now is the time to trust what you have practiced. You've learned proper alignment and the set. You have acquired a good pre-shot pattern. You have practiced the swing. Now you have to let it all happen and leave the shot to take care of itself. With that thought in mind, here are the steps you should go through mentally before every shot:

1. Think the shot through. Pick your target and note such conditions as terrain and wind that will determine your choice of club.

2. Having selected your club, look first at the ball and then the target, forming a mental image of the swing and the shot you want to make. Make this as vivid as possible.

3. Go into your pre-shot pattern.

4. Swing!

Obitz and Farley Say:

1. Every golfer is actually two people. One is the "practicer," the other is the "player." Don't confuse the two.

2. To know where your game stands now, analyze your rounds to find your strengths and weaknesses. Have pictures taken of your swing.

3. Always practice with a purpose. Aimless practice is useless practice.

4. Before a round, make your game plan and warm up mind and muscle.

5. When you're playing the game, keep your mind on what's important—the next shot.